The Kitchens of Biró
Simple SpanAsian Cuisine

Marcel Biró and Shannon Kring Biró
Photographs by Marty Snortum

Gibbs Smith, Publisher
TO ENRICH AND INSPIRE HUMANKIND
Salt Lake City | Charleston | Santa Fe | Santa Barbara

First Edition
11 10 09 08 07   5 4 3 2 1

Published by
Gibbs Smith, Publisher
P.O. Box 667
Layton, Utah 84041

Orders: 1.800.835.4993
www.gibbs-smith.com
www.birointernationale.com

Designed by Debra McQuiston
Food Styling by Marcel Biró
Set Styling by Katie Beck
Printed and bound in China

Library of Congress Cataloging-in-Publication Data

Biró, Marcel.
  The kitchens of Biró : simple SpanAsian cuisine / Marcel Biró and Shannon Kring Biró ; photographs by Marty Snortum. — 1st ed.
      p. cm.
  Originally published: New York : Van Nostrand Reinhold, c1991.
  ISBN-13: 978-1-4236-0117-3
  ISBN-10: 1-4236-0117-3
  1. Ó (Restaurant) 2. Cookery, Spanish. 3. Cookery, Asian. I. Biró, Shannon Kring. II. Title.

TX723.5.S7B55 2007
641.5'946—dc22
                    2006026576

We wish to thank . . .

Heather Blamey, for always working as hard as we do. We're grateful for your dedication, loyalty, and friendship.

Lawrence Turcotte, for providing the beverage pairings for this book. You're the soul of Biró Restaurant and Wine Bar.

Raul Morales, for assisting with the tapas recipes, and Grayson Schmitz, for transcribing them. Raul, your positive attitude and warm smile make Ó as great a place to work as it is to eat.

Marilyn McCallum, Ann Blamey, Eileen Sherman, Susan Nenning, Pat Hamilton, Tina Rettler, Bill Moren, and Anne Sprecher, for their recipe testing expertise.

Cathy Fowler, for believing in us and being so much more than an agent. We love you.

Suzanne Taylor, Alison Einerson, Jennifer Grillone, and everyone else at Gibbs Smith, for giving us our break and two stunning cookbooks.

Marty Snortum, for giving us two of the most beautifully photographed cookbooks and plenty of laughs.

Jeff Buser and Mike Beeck, for helping us make our flagship Ó such a beautiful place, and Robert Rauh, for his advice and friendship.

Erika Helbig, Rita Biró, Nicole and Michael Zeune, Sandra Kring, Kerry Kring, Natalie Kring, Neil Kring, and Jerry Ducommun, for their incredible support and for understanding our crazy lifestyles.

Without all of you, we wouldn't be able to do what we love. Thank you!

Contents

Welcome to Ó!

It was Marcel who dreamed up Ó. "Let's open a restaurant with Spanish and Asian food. SpanAsian," he said to me in the spring of 2004.

"Sure, let's do that. And write the *Biró: European-Inspired Cuisine* cookbook. And launch *The Kitchens of Biró*. And run Biró Restaurant and Wine Bar. And Marcel Biró Culinary School. Oh, and let's not forget our consulting. Sounds great," I said, not bothering to look up from my computer screen.

The problem was, Marcel really did think it sounded great. We'd be in the middle of a television production meeting, and he'd be crunching numbers. I'd ask him if he puts two teaspoons or two tablespoons of glace de viande in his Cognac Crème Sauce, and he'd answer that Spice-Rubbed Andalusian Steak with Rock Shrimp would be great on the Ó menu. Sleep was soon shooed to the back burner, as it interfered with his obsession.

Like a parent who succumbs to tearful pleading in the candy aisle, I grudgingly agreed to open Ó. Five weeks later—three days before we welcomed

500 people to the premiere of *The Kitchens of Biró*, and just a few short weeks before our first cookbook manuscript was due—our doors were open.

Ó is where the elegant simplicity of Asian cuisine meets the straightforward rusticity of Spanish fare, where earthy tapas and colorful sushi take their place on the table next to crispy tarte flambées and simply luxurious miso. Our approach makes high-quality, seasonal food accessible and translates to an unforgettable upscale-casual dining experience in a contemporary setting.

The design of the restaurant and bar evoke and draw upon images from both Asia and Spain, with sleek stainless, angled blonde hardwoods and vibrant red and yellow wall treatments. Amber and orange valance lighting is enhanced by white Asian lanterns over the bar and by glowing candelas on the tables. The tableware is both streamlined and rustic, and hand-hammered stainless steel decorative accents add interest.

The stunning outdoor patio, like our

cuisine, marries Spanish and Asian nuances—weeping juniper and bamboo, terra-cotta pots and smooth stones—and as I said to Marcel on opening night, "It all works."

And does it ever work when it comes to Ó's cuisine! Baby Calamari Salad with Olive Oil, Garlic, Parsley, White Wine & Lemon; LaMancha Pasta with Lamb Ragoût; Sautéed Vegetables & Red Wine; Lamb Cracklings with Cabrales Cheese & Honey; Salmon Teriyaki Satay with Garlic-Fried Rice & Mixed Greens Salad; Hojiblanca Olive Cake with Olive Oil Ice Cream are just a few of Ó's simple recipes that yield profound flavor. Here, they're presented in a book that's much like the restaurant itself: Welcoming. Stylish. Laid-back. The kind of place you'll keep coming back to.

"Let's take the Ó concept national," Marcel said shortly after opening.

I looked around the crowded dining room. Laughter, Spanish music, and the luscious aromas of garlic, cinnamon, and seafood filled the air.

"Sounds great," I said, and meant it.
— Shannon Kring Biró

SpanAsian® Cuisine

Metric Conversion Chart

Liquid and Dry Measures

U.S.	Canadian	Australian
$\frac{1}{4}$ teaspoon	1 mL	1 ml
$\frac{1}{2}$ teaspoon	2 mL	2 ml
1 teaspoon	5 mL	5 ml
1 Tablespoon	15 mL	20 ml
$\frac{1}{4}$ cup	50 mL	60 ml
$\frac{1}{3}$ cup	75 mL	80 ml
$\frac{1}{2}$ cup	125 mL	125 ml
$\frac{2}{3}$ cup	150 mL	170 ml
$\frac{3}{4}$ cup	175 mL	190 ml
1 cup	250 mL	250 ml
1 quart	1 liter	1 litre

Temperature Conversion Chart

Fahrenheit	Celsius
250	120
275	140
300	150
325	160
350	180
375	190
400	200
425	220
450	230
475	240
500	260

About Cooking with Us

The following information is helpful when preparing the recipes in this book.

Ingredients. High-quality ingredients yield high-quality results. Read past the calorie and fat content on labels to see if what you're putting in your dishes is good for the preparation and, more importantly, for you. When possible, purchase organic and free-range items. Make certain that your dairy products are not laden with fillers. Cream should contain at least 40 percent milk fat. Butter should be unsalted. Olive oil, which is called for throughout this book, should be from the first cold press and contain olives from only one country of origin. Flour should be unbleached, and you should discard any unused portion after three months. (Flour absorbs moisture, so after time it yields heavy and flat results.) Salt should come from the sea, as earth-mined salts are refined and thus don't have as pure a flavor. You need to use only 1 teaspoon sea salt to 1 tablespoon earth-mined salt.

Tools, Cookware & Appliances. Though some of the recipes contained within this book call for special tools such as a chinois, the tools most important to own for all home and professional chefs is a good knife or two, and some high-quality cookware. A knife should fit comfortably in your hand. It should not be too big for your fingers to completely wrap around, but also not so small that it gets lost in your palm and prevents you from keeping a firm grip at all times. It should be well balanced and have a full tang. All cookware should be heavy. Aluminum-core clad and copper cookware is best. Home appliances are becoming more and more like those found in professional kitchens, which is great. These recipes were adapted for home gas ranges.

Tableware & Tabletop Décor. All tableware and tabletop décor should reflect your personal style, but also play a supporting role to the star: your food. We use simple white dishes, as they best show off our creations. Flowers should not be overpowering in fragrance. Candles should be unscented.

Beverage Pairings. We know that pairing wine with food can be an intimidating process for some. While there are basic guidelines for wine service—red wine with red meat, white wine with fish—the most important thing to remember is that you should drink what you like. To make things easier, we've provided you with beverage pairings for every recipe contained within this book, and we encourage you to experiment with other varietals as well.

Specifics. Unless otherwise noted, all herbs are fresh. All flour is all-purpose. All sugar is granulated. All items that would normally be peeled—such as garlic and onions—are.

Soups**&**Salads

Misó with Glass Noodles, Scallions & Mushrooms

Miso is fermented soybean paste. It is used widely in Japanese cooking, both as a flavoring agent and as a condiment. Look for lighter-colored (and thus milder) varieties for use in delicate soups and sauces, and darker varieties for more substantial dishes.

For this soup, we slice the vegetables thinly, and then ladle the hot liquid over them. In a matter of seconds, they'll be cooked to perfection.

---

5 cups Chicken Stock (see page 152)
2 tablespoons sliced pickled sushi-style ginger
6 tablespoons miso
2 leaves kombu
1 (1-ounce) package glass noodles
2 tablespoons soy sauce
2 tablespoons diced shallots
2 tablespoons sliced scallions
4 ounces enoki mushrooms
8 ounces shiitake mushrooms, thinly sliced
6 ounces firm tofu, diced
Sesame oil for garnish

1 Combine the stock, ginger, miso, and kombu in a medium stockpot over high heat, and bring to a boil. Reduce heat to low, and skim any impurities that have risen to the surface during the cooking process.

2 Simmer for 15 minutes, and then add the glass noodles and soy sauce. Let stand for 1 minute.

[SERVES 8]

PRESENTATION

Place the shallots, scallions, mushrooms, and tofu in serving dishes. We like to arrange the two types of mushrooms opposite one another to create balance. Ladle the hot liquid over the vegetables and tofu. Drizzle with the sesame oil.

BEVERAGE PAIRINGS

Hakutsuru Sake
"Junmai Dai Ginjo"
Kobe, Japan

Mont-Marçal
Brut "Extremarium"
Penedés, Spain

Garlic Soup with Manchego Cheese Croûton

When we talk about the rustic simplicity of the Spanish-inspired dishes at Ó, we're talking about offerings such as this that use few ingredients but are packed with flavor.

For a more intense, earthy flavor, we prefer washing the garlic heads and onions, but not peeling them. Cut them in half and prepare the recipe as directed, pressing the garlic and onions with a silicone spatula or the back of a wooden spoon to extract all the flavor during the milling process. Discard the solids.

6 slices baguette, ½ inch thick
½ cup grated Manchego cheese
4 tablespoons unsalted butter
4 heads garlic, peeled and crushed
2 yellow onions, finely chopped
4 tablespoons flour
1 quart heavy cream, cold
1 quart whole milk, cold
Sea salt
Freshly ground white pepper
Coarsely chopped parsley for garnish

1 Heat the oven to 400 degrees F.

2 Place the baguette slices on a baking sheet lined with Silpat or parchment paper. Sprinkle with the cheese, and bake for 4 to 5 minutes, or until lightly toasted.

3 Melt the butter in a large saucepan over medium heat. Add the garlic and onions, and sauté until lightly golden brown.

4 Make a roux by stirring in the flour. Stir in the cold cream and milk, and bring to a boil. Cook, stirring frequently, until the flour taste is cooked out, about 15 minutes. Remove from heat.

5 Pass the soup through a food mill. Pour the milled soup through a chinois or fine-mesh sieve, and season with salt and pepper.

[SERVES 6]

PRESENTATION

Pour the soup into serving dishes, and top with a croûton. Garnish with the parsley. Garlic Soup with Manchego Cheese Croûton is fantastic served with crusty bread.

BEVERAGE PAIRINGS

Dr. Burklin-Wolf Riesling Estate
Pfalz, Germany

Palacio de Menade
Verdejo
Rueda, Spain

Roasted Potato Soup with Chorizo

Chorizo is a flavorful pork sausage that's seasoned with garlic, chile, and pimentón, and is available in mild, hot, and sweet varieties. Traditional Spanish chorizo is made with chopped (often smoked) pork, and Mexican chorizo—which is much more readily available in the United States—is usually made with fresh ground pork. If chorizo is not available, you can substitute hot ground Italian sausage. This soup is also great without meat, and you can use Vegetable Stock (see page 153) for a completely vegetarian presentation.

---

4 ounces chorizo, casings removed
2 tablespoons extra virgin olive oil
2 tablespoons unsalted butter
2 yellow onions, diced
2 carrots, peeled and diced
1 stalk celery, diced
1 leek, white and light green parts only, diced
2½ pounds Yukon Gold potatoes, unpeeled and diced
6 cups Chicken Stock (see page 152)
2 tablespoons chopped marjoram
4 tablespoons chopped parsley, divided
Sea salt
Freshly ground black pepper

1 Brown the chorizo in a small sauté pan over high heat. Drain.

2 Heat the oil and butter in a large stockpot over medium-high heat. Add the onions, carrots, celery, and leek, and sauté until tender but not brown, about 5 minutes. Add the potatoes, and sauté for 2 additional minutes.

3 Pour in the stock, and reduce heat to low; bring to a boil. Cook until the potatoes begin to break apart. Add the marjoram and 3 tablespoons parsley, and season with salt and pepper. Remove from heat.

4 Process the soup in a food processor or blender until it reaches the desired consistency. We purée ours slightly so that it's creamy but there are still some small potato pieces that give the soup texture. If it is too thick for your liking, thin it out with a little more stock.

[S E R V E S   4]

PRESENTATION

Pour the soup into serving dishes. Place a small mound of chorizo in the center of each serving, and sprinkle with the remaining parsley.

BEVERAGE PAIRINGS

Hidalgo-Pastrana Manzanilla Pasada
Sanlúcar de Barrameda, Spain

Penascal
Blanco
Castilla y Leon, Spain

Hot & Sour Chicken Soup

This quick and delicious recipe uses a high-quality canned hot-and-sour soup mix containing potato starch, black fungus, carrot, cabbage, cilantro, soy sauce, and white pepper. You can find good mixes that do not contain MSG in Asian grocery stores and online.

You may use button mushrooms or an assortment of fresh, wild, or exotic mushrooms in this recipe. Our Pesto-Marinated Chicken Breast (see page 155) adds flavor, but you could use plain diced chicken.

---

1 (16-ounce) can hot-and-sour soup mix
2 quarts water
1¼ ounces dried black fungus
2 cups thinly sliced mushrooms
**3 tablespoons diced Pesto-Marinated Chicken Breast
    (see page 155)**
2 tablespoons sliced scallions

Pour the hot-and-sour soup mix into a large stockpot. Add the water and fungus, and bring to a boil over high heat, whisking frequently.

[SERVES 4]

PRESENTATION

Place the mushrooms and chicken in serving dishes. Ladle the soup over the mushrooms and chicken, and garnish with the scallions.

BEVERAGE PAIRINGS

Legar de Cervera-Albariño
Rias Baixas, Spain

Palacios Remondo
Blanca Placet
Rioja Baja, Spain

Gazpacho

Originally a laborers' dish, gazpacho was the standard fare of Andalusian muleteers who carried it in earthen pots on their travels. Today the soup contains vegetables and differs from city to city within Andalusia—each version claiming to be the original. Arguably, the first recipe came from Córdoba and consisted of bread, garlic, olive oil, and water. Today Córdoban gazpacho is thickened with cream and cornmeal. In Jerez it is garnished with raw onion rings, and in Malaga it is made with veal bouillon and sometimes garnished with grapes and almonds. In Cadiz gazpacho is served hot in the winter, and in Segovia it is flavored with cumin, basil, and aïoli.

This recipe is inspired by that of Seville, a city that, of course, also lays claim as home of gazpacho.

---

1 pound vine-ripened tomatoes, peeled and chopped
½ cucumber, peeled and chopped
1 green bell pepper, seeded and chopped
1 red bell pepper, seeded and chopped
1 small yellow onion, chopped
1 clove garlic, chopped
1 cup breadcrumbs
2 tablespoons extra virgin olive oil
2 tablespoons red wine vinegar
2 cups tomato juice
½ teaspoon dried leaf marjoram
Sea salt
Freshly ground black pepper

1   Place all ingredients in a food processor or blender, and process until the soup reaches the desired consistency. Some people prefer chunks, others a completely smooth soup. We like our Gazpacho somewhere in the middle: with small chunks and the consistency of heavy cream.

2   Pour the soup into a large stainless steel bowl, cover, and refrigerate for at least 2 hours. When the soup is well chilled, adjust seasoning with salt and pepper.

[SERVES 6]

PRESENTATION

Gazpacho is traditionally served with a selection of garnishes including chopped hard-boiled eggs, chopped cucumber, chopped onion, chopped green and black olives, and diced green bell pepper. This soup is therefore best served family style, and we prefer to use earthenware dishes, as the recipe was originally prepared in clay bowls.

BEVERAGE PAIRINGS

Castaño
Solanera
Yecla, Spain

Burgans
Albariño
Rias Baixas, Spain

Quick Tip: Other Uses for Gazpacho

We've used gazpacho leftovers as a pizza sauce, a warm pasta sauce, a sauce for a goat cheese tarte flambée, a cold and warm garnish, and even as a cocktail sauce by adding a bit of horseradish. Be inventive with this versatile soup and know that the longer you keep it, the more complex and intense its flavor will become.

Saffron Shrimp-Leek Soup

As in many other soups and stocks using shrimp, we use unpeeled shrimp in the preparation of this recipe. Leaving the shells on gives the dish an intense flavor the shrimp itself could not produce. You may wish to add 2 tablespoons dry white wine to the leeks while sautéing to further enhance this soup's earthy but refined flavor.

¼ cup unsalted butter
1 pound (16 to 20) shrimp, unpeeled
4 threads saffron
4 large leeks, white and light green parts only, chopped
3 cups Fish Stock (see page 153)
2 cups heavy cream
2 teaspoons sea salt
½ teaspoon freshly ground white pepper

1   Melt the butter in a medium sauté pan over high heat. Add the shrimp and saffron, and sauté until the shrimp become pink, about 2 minutes. Do not allow the shrimp to brown, or they will be chewy. Remove the shrimp from the pan, and bring the pan back up to high heat. Add the leeks, and sauté for 30 seconds.

2   Add enough stock to cover the leeks by about 1½ inches. Bring the stock to a simmer, and cook gently until the leeks are tender, about 8 minutes. Remove from heat and allow to cool slightly.

3   Peel and devein the shrimp, discarding the shells.

4   Place the cooled soup in a food processor or blender and then process until smooth. Strain through a chinois or fine-mesh sieve into a clean pan over low heat.

5   Stir in the cream. Simmer until the soup is thickened, about 5 minutes. Add the shrimp, and season with salt and pepper.

[S E R V E S 8]

P R E S E N T A T I O N

Ladle into serving dishes, and serve immediately.

BEVERAGE PAIRINGS

Hidalgo Amontillado Napoleon
Sanlúcar de Barrameda, Spain

Bodegas Angel Rodriguez
Martinsancho Verdejo
Rueda, Spain

Quick Tip: About Saffron

Saffron is the type of ingredient that at mere mention makes gourmands salivate and debate and kitchen novices perspire and quake. We've seen both happen at our culinary school. "The best saffron's from Spain! I paid $60 for a thimble-sized jar of it just the other day!" a foodie may pipe, while someone at the back of the classroom may be wondering, "What is saffron? If it costs that much, I don't think I even want to know."

Here's the deal on saffron: it's a pungent, slightly bitter spice that comes from the dried stigmas of the saffron crocus plant. It is available in yellow-orange powder or burnt-orange thread forms and originated in the East. Whether you find saffron from Spain, Italy, Greece, Turkey, Morocco, or somewhere else, it's expensive. This is because it takes around 85,000 stigmas to create just over a pound of saffron.

The good news is because of saffron's strength, a little goes a long way in flavoring and adding color to soups, stocks, risotto, paella, meats, vegetables, and desserts. But if you don't want to spring for the real thing, no problem. Simply substitute safflower, called "bastard saffron," or turmeric, called "Indian saffron."

Serrano Ham Soup with Garlic & Manchego

Like many Spanish country soups, this one features ham, chopped hard-boiled eggs, sweet pimentón, and bread.

¼ cup extra virgin olive oil
1 tablespoon unsalted butter
4 slices baguette, ½ inch thick
5 ounces Serrano ham, diced
6 cups Chicken Stock (see page 152)
4 cloves garlic, minced
Freshly ground black pepper
1 teaspoon sweet pimentón
Sea salt
½ cup shredded Manchego cheese
2 large hard-boiled eggs, chopped
1 tablespoon chopped flat-leaf parsley

1 Heat the oil and butter in a stockpot over high heat. Sauté the baguette slices until golden on both sides. Remove the baguette slices, and reserve the remaining oil and butter.

2 Return the pot to high heat. Add the ham, and sauté for 1 minute. Add the stock, garlic, pepper, and pimentón. Bring to a boil. Season with salt, and reduce heat to medium. Cover, and simmer for 30 minutes.

[SERVES 4]

PRESENTATION

Heat the broiler. Pour the soup into ovenproof dishes, and top with a baguette slice. Sprinkle with the cheese. Broil for 1 to 2 minutes, or until the cheese is bubbly and golden brown. Sprinkle with the egg and parsley, and serve immediately.

BEVERAGE PAIRINGS

Bodegas Godeval
Godeval Blanco (100% Godello)
Valdeorras, Spain

Bodegas Bretón Criadores, S.L.
Loriñon Blanco
Rioja, Spain

Mixed Greens Salad with Feta, Sun-Dried Tomatoes & Spanish Olives

This is such a simple salad to make that you might be surprised at just how beautiful and tasty it is. It's great on its own and versatile enough to be served with any of the Spanish- or Asian-inspired main dishes found in this book.

---

24 ounces mixed greens
1 cup Feta cheese, diced
¼ cup Spanish olives
¼ cup sun-dried tomatoes, julienned
1 small yellow onion, thinly sliced
½ cup Ó House Dressing (see page 156)

▬▬▬▬▬▬▬

Place the greens, cheese, olives, tomatoes, and onion in a large, chilled stainless steel bowl. Drizzle evenly with the dressing, and mix gently but thoroughly to combine.

[S E R V E S   8]

P R E S E N T A T I O N
Place in serving dishes, and serve with crusty bread.

B E V E R A G E   P A I R I N G S
Domeca La Ina
Dry Fino Sherry
Jerez, Spain

Abadia Retuerta
Primicia
Sardon del Duero, Spain

▬▬▬▬▬▬▬

Quick Tip: Get Your Hands Dirty!

We've already given this tip on *The Kitchens of Biró* television series, and in the *Biró: European-Inspired Cuisine* cookbook. But it's so important, we're giving it to you again here!

When coating leaves with dressing, we do it by hand, so we can feel that the dressing has properly made contact with each green, imparting its flavor throughout the dish. Using tongs can damage the leaves, causing them to "bleed" and become mushy.

Asian Cucumber Salad with Red Onions, Roasted Sweet Peppers & Yogurt-Dill Vinaigrette

This one-of-a kind salad bursts with flavor and eye-dazzling color. With red onion, pickled ginger, and a dash of our zesty SpanAsian Seasoning Mix, it's also got a bit of kick.

2 medium hothouse cucumbers, peeled and thinly sliced
1 teaspoon sea salt
¼ cup Ó Asian Dressing (see page 156)
1 tablespoon Ó Yogurt-Dill Vinaigrette (see page 154)
1 small red onion, julienned
2 teaspoons sliced pickled sushi-style ginger
2 teaspoons sliced scallions
8 ounces mixed greens
1 tablespoon Ó House Dressing (see page 156)
1 tablespoon julienned roasted red bell pepper
Ó SpanAsian Seasoning Mix (see page 158) for garnish
Black sesame seeds for garnish

1 Place the cucumber slices in a bowl, and sprinkle with the salt. Refrigerate for 30 minutes to remove any excess water. Drain the saltwater.

2 Add the Ó Asian Dressing to the cucumbers, and toss gently to coat. Divide the coated cucumbers evenly among serving dishes. Top with a dollop of the Ó Yogurt-Dill Vinaigrette. Sprinkle with the onion, ginger, and scallions.

[SERVES 4]

PRESENTATION

Place the greens in a large bowl, and toss gently with the Ó House Dressing. Place a small mound of coated greens beside the cucumbers. Top with the bell pepper. Garnish with the Ó SpanAsian Seasoning Mix and sesame seeds. Serve immediately.

BEVERAGE PAIRINGS

Can Feixes
Blanc Selecció
Penedés, Spain

Christmann
Idig-Königsbach
Pfalz, Germany

Garlic-Grilled Octopus & Seaweed Salad

Octopus has the texture of escargot and a flavor similar to prawns. Ask your fishmonger to separate the octopus for you, as the cartilage in the head is difficult to remove on your own. If you're not able to locate octopus, substitute calamari, prawns, or ahi tuna.

You can prepare the octopus a day in advance. Bring to room temperature before proceeding with the rest of the recipe. The vinaigrette tastes best if made the day before, as it allows the flavors to infuse.

OCTOPUS

1 (2-pound) octopus, separated
¼ cup extra virgin olive oil
Pinch of red pepper flakes
2 cloves garlic, chopped
1 vine-ripened red tomato, cut into thin wedges
1 large vine-ripened yellow tomato, cut into thin wedges
1 large Vidalia onion, coarsely sliced
Sea salt
Freshly ground black pepper

SEAWEED SALAD

¾ ounce dried wakame seaweed, shredded
3 tablespoons rice vinegar
3 tablespoons soy sauce
2 tablespoons sesame oil
1 teaspoon sugar
1 teaspoon freshly grated ginger
1 clove garlic, minced
1 Granny Smith apple, julienned
2 scallions, thinly sliced
2 tablespoons chopped cilantro

DISH

1 tablespoon chopped mint leaves for garnish
1 tablespoon toasted white sesame seeds for garnish

---

1   To make the octopus, preheat oven to 350 degrees F.

2   Brush the octopus with the oil, and then rub with the red pepper flakes and garlic. Transfer the octopus to a baking sheet, and bake for 30 to 35 minutes, or until tender and purple in color. You'll know the octopus is done when you can easily cut through the thickest part of a tentacle.

3   Heat a grill or grill pan to high heat. Grill the octopus until lightly charred. Allow to cool slightly, and then chop into bite-sized pieces.

4   Place the tomatoes and onion on the grill or grill pan, and grill until the tomatoes have softened and the onion is translucent. Add to the octopus mixture, and toss gently to combine. Season with salt and pepper.

5   To make the seaweed salad, soak the seaweed in warm water to cover for 5 minutes. Drain, and then squeeze out the excess water.

6   To make the vinaigrette, whisk together the vinegar, soy sauce, oil, sugar, ginger, and garlic in a small bowl. Add the octopus, seaweed, apple, scallions, and cilantro, and mix well to combine.

[S E R V E S   6]

PRESENTATION

Place the salad in serving dishes, and garnish with the mint and sesame seeds.

BEVERAGE PAIRINGS

Usco Albariño
Rias Baixas, Spain

Bodegas Angel Rodriguez
Martinsancho Verdejo
Rueda, Spain

Sautéed Shrimp or Baby Calamari Salad with Olive Oil, Garlic, Parsley, White Wine & Lemon

This dish combines Spanish flavor with Asian nuances, resulting in a brightly flavored salad substantial enough to be served as a main course. You may use shrimp or calamari as the main ingredient. Experiment with both and decide which you like best. Both variations yield equally delicious but distinct flavors.

¼ cup extra virgin olive oil
½ pound rock shrimp or ½ pound sliced baby calamari
2 tablespoons sliced garlic
1 tablespoon dry white wine
1 tablespoon Ó SpanAsian Seasoning Mix (see page 158)
1 tablespoon lemon juice
1 tablespoon chopped flat-leaf parsley
24 ounces mixed greens
¼ cup Ó House Dressing (see page 156)
¼ cup Ó Asian Dressing (see page 156)
¼ cup sun-dried tomatoes, julienned
½ small yellow onion, thinly sliced

1   Heat the oil in a large sauté pan over high heat. Add the shrimp or calamari and the garlic, and sauté until the garlic is glossy and the seafood is cooked through, about 2 minutes. Add the wine. Remove from heat, and season with the Ó SpanAsian Seasoning Mix and lemon juice. Sprinkle with the parsley.

2   In a large bowl, gently toss the mixed greens with the Ó House and Asian Dressings. Add the tomatoes and onion, and toss.

[S E R V E S   4]

PRESENTATION

Place the greens in serving dishes, and top with the sautéed shrimp or calamari.

BEVERAGE PAIRINGS

Hidalgo La Gitana Mazanilla
Sanlúcar de Barrameda, Spain

Bodegas González Lara
Fuente del Conte
Rosado de Tempranillo
Cigales, Spain

Chilled Calanda Peach Soup with Ibérico Ham

Calanda peaches from the lower Aragon region of Spain have been renowned since medieval times. Today, they're protected by the Melocotón de Calanda Denomonation of Origin, a designation similar to that given to wines or olive oils from a particular region. Currently, forty-five towns produce them. If Calanda peaches are not available, you may use any sweet, fleshy variety or use high-quality canned peaches in light syrup for this recipe.

2½ pounds fresh Calanda peaches, plus more for garnish
2 tablespoons extra virgin olive oil, divided
5 ounces Ibérico ham, julienned
1 leek, white part only, julienned
1 small yellow onion, diced
3¼ cups Chicken Stock (see page 152)
Sea salt
Freshly ground white pepper
Freshly ground nutmeg
Ground cinnamon
½ cup half-and-half
Mint leaves for garnish

1   Wash the peaches. Cut in half, and remove the pits. Dice.

2   Heat 1 tablespoon olive oil in a stockpot over high heat. Add the ham, and sauté until crispy. Drain on paper towel.

3   Return the pot to high heat. Add the remaining oil. Add the leek and onion, and sauté until glossy, about 1 minute. Add the peaches, and sauté for 1 additional minute.

4   Add the stock. Season with the salt, pepper, nutmeg, and cinnamon. Reduce heat to low. Cover, and simmer for 10 minutes.

5   Allow the soup to cool slightly, and then process in a food processor or blender until smooth.

6   Return the soup to the pot, and warm over high heat. Stir in the half-and-half, and then bring to a boil. Adjust seasoning as necessary. Refrigerate for at least 2 hours prior to serving. Adjust seasoning as necessary.

[SERVES 8]

PRESENTATION

Dice 1 peach. Pour the soup into serving dishes. Garnish with the sautéed ham, peach dices, and mint. Serve immediately.

BEVERAGE PAIRINGS

Muga Blanco
Rioja, Spain

Lustau
Manzanilla Papirusa
Jerez, Spain

Quick Tip: Getting the Most Punch from Your Peach

Have you ever taken a bite from a peach that looked fantastic but then yielded a disappointing, nearly non-existent flavor? It's not necessarily the fruit's ripeness or quality that's to blame. It could be your refrigerator. After purchase, peaches should be placed in a plastic bag and refrigerated for up to 5 days. Before eating, however, peaches should be brought to room temperature. This releases the peach's juices and softens the flesh, which will release all that succulent flavor you're looking for.

Apple Salad with Toasted Spanish Almonds, Honey-Herb Vinaigrette & Torta del Casar Cheese

This is a simple and delicious salad that perfectly captures the flavor of sun-drenched Spain. The vinaigrette is also wonderful used as a marinade for grilled chicken breast.

If Marcona almonds are not available, use any almond you wish.

¼ **cup lemon juice**

2 **tablespoons honey**

½ **teaspoon Dijon mustard**

1 **clove garlic, minced**

½ **teaspoon minced parsley**

¼ **teaspoon sea salt**

⅛ **teaspoon freshly ground black pepper**

¼ **cup extra virgin olive oil**

1 **Granny Smith apple, cored and julienned**

6 **ounces Torta del Casar cheese, crumbled**

½ **cup toasted Marcona almonds**

6 **cups torn romaine lettuce**

━━━━━━━━━━━

1   To make the vinaigrette, combine the lemon juice, honey, mustard, garlic, and parsley in a small bowl. Season with salt and pepper. Slowly whisk in the oil to emulsify. Let the vinaigrette rest for at least 15 minutes so that the flavors infuse, and then adjust seasoning as necessary.

2   To make the salad, place the apple, cheese, almonds, and lettuce in a large bowl. Drizzle with the vinaigrette, and gently toss to coat.

[S E R V E S   6]

PRESENTATION

Place in serving dishes, and serve with crusty bread.

BEVERAGE PAIRINGS

Morgadio Albariño
Rias Baixas, Spain

Viña Reboreda
Gran Reboreda
Ribeiro, Spain

Noodles&Tartes

Glass Noodle Salad with Scallions, Red Pepper Flakes, Sesame Dressing & Grilled Salmon

Guests who try this inventive sweet-and-spicy salad keep coming back to it. Vegetarians order it without the salmon, and many guests swear by the spice-rubbed steak variation, below. We serve it in generous bowls with soy sauce and chopsticks.

Glass noodles are also called cellophane noodles or bean threads. They're translucent and made from the starch of green mung beans. You can find them in most grocery stores and in all Asian markets.

Soak the bamboo skewers in water for a minimum of 10 minutes before grilling to prevent the wood from burning.

---

4 (1-ounce) packages glass noodles
½ cup Ó Asian Dressing (see page 156)
1 pound salmon, sliced into 8 pieces
2 tablespoons extra virgin olive oil
Sea salt
Freshly ground black pepper
8 ounces mixed greens
2 tablespoons Ó House Dressing (see page 156)
1 tablespoon sliced pickled sushi-style ginger
Black sesame seeds
1 tablespoon red pepper flakes
1 tablespoon sliced scallions

1 Bring a medium pot of water to a boil. Blanch the glass noodles until clear, about 3 minutes. Drain, and rinse under cold water. Allow to dry, and then place in a large bowl. Add Ó Asian Dressing, and toss well to coat.
2 Heat a grill or grill pan.
3 Thread the salmon pieces onto bamboo skewers. Drizzle with the oil, and season with salt and pepper. Grill, turning once, until medium-rare, about 1 minute on each side.

[S E R V E S 4]

PRESENTATION

Place the coated glass noodles in serving dishes. In a large bowl, gently toss together the mixed greens and Ó House Dressing. Place a small mound of coated greens in each dish. Top with 2 salmon skewers each, and garnish with the ginger, sesame seeds, red pepper flakes, and scallions. Serve immediately with soy sauce.

BEVERAGE PAIRINGS

Gunderloch Estate
Dry Riesling
Rheinhessen, Germany

Lieser Estate
Reisling Kabinett
Mosel, Germany

Quick Tip: Steak Variation

You can substitute 4 ounces steak in this recipe and prepare it the same way as the salmon.

Andalusian "Pesta"

Consistently one of the most often-ordered dishes at Ó, Andalusian "Pesta" is a flavorful pasta dish made with pesto, mushrooms, Spanish seasoning, and two melted cheeses. For variation, add sautéed rock shrimp, as many of our guests do. You may also wish to try it with sautéed or grilled chicken breast.

1 (16-ounce) box dried cellentani pasta
½ cup extra virgin olive oil
¼ cup sliced garlic
3 cups sliced button mushrooms
¼ cup Pesto (see page 155)
1 cup Velouté (see page 155)
¼ cup Ó SpanAsian Seasoning Mix (see page 158)
½ cup freshly grated Parmesan cheese
1½ cups grated mozzarella cheese
Chopped flat-leaf parsley for garnish

1 Prepare the pasta according to the package instructions.

2 Heat the oil in a very large sauté pan over high heat. Add the garlic and mushrooms, and sauté until the garlic is lightly golden and the mushrooms are softened, 1 to 2 minutes. Add the Pesto, and stir until well combined. Stir in the Velouté and Ó SpanAsian Seasoning Mix.

3 Add the pasta to heat through. Add the Parmesan cheese, and toss well to coat.

[SERVES 4]

PRESENTATION

Place in serving dishes and top with the mozzarella cheese. Garnish with the parsley.

BEVERAGE PAIRINGS

Lustau Amontillada Los Arcos
Jerez, Spain

Vina Alarba
Old Vines Grenache
Calatayud, Spain

Macaroni & Cheese

This is comfort food, Biró style, and is a hit with kids and adults of all ages. For variation, you could sprinkle with sautéed breadcrumbs, and then place under the broiler to finish.

---

1 (16-ounce) box dried cellentani pasta
2 cups Velouté (see page 155)
6 cups grated mozzarella cheese
2½ cups freshly grated Parmesan cheese, plus more for garnish
Sea salt
Freshly ground white pepper
Chopped flat-leaf parsley for garnish

━━━━━━━━━━━

1   Prepare the pasta according to the package instructions.

2   Heat the Velouté in a very large saucepan over medium-high heat until it just comes to a boil. Add the cheeses, and stir until melted.

3   Add the pasta to heat through; toss well to coat. Season with salt and pepper.

[SERVES 8]

PRESENTATION

Place in serving dishes, and garnish with the parsley. Serve immediately.

BEVERAGE PAIRINGS

Viña Sila "Naia"
Rueda, Spain

Especial Reserva
Pilsner Lager
Spanish Beer

━━━━━━━━━━━

Quick Tip: Serrano Ham Variation

Unlike hams in other countries, Spanish hams are carved with the grain and have flavorful fat running through them. As you can tell, we love Serrano ham, which is salted for four to ten days, and then hung to dry for about six months.

For variation, you may wish to sauté 4 ounces of Serrano ham in 2 teaspoons olive oil, and add it in step 3.

LaMancha Pasta with Lamb Ragoût, Sautéed Vegetables & Red Wine

This is a hearty pasta that perfectly reflects the rusticity of traditional Spanish fare. It's especially wonderful served in autumn.

1 (16-ounce) box dried campanelle pasta
4 cups Lamb Ragoût (see page 159)
¼ cup Velouté (see page 155)
2 cups freshly grated Parmesan cheese
1½ cups fresh sweet peas
Sea salt
Freshly ground black pepper
1 cup grated Manchego cheese
1 tablespoon chopped cilantro for garnish

1   Prepare the pasta according to the package instructions.
2   Heat the Lamb Ragoût and Velouté in a very large sauté pan over high heat until it just comes to a boil. Stir in the Parmesan cheese and peas.
3   Add the pasta to heat through; toss well to coat.

Season with salt and pepper.

[SERVES 4]

PRESENTATION

Place in serving dishes, and top with the Manchego cheese. Garnish with the cilantro.

BEVERAGE PAIRINGS

Dehesa la Granja
Ribera del Duero, Spain

Tinto Pesquera Reserva
Ribera del Duero, Spain

Serrano Ham, Manchego, Tomato & Salad Double-Decker Tarte Flambée

Tarte Flambée, also called Flammkuchen, is an Alsatian specialty that resembles an extremely thin-crust pizza and translates to "flame cake" because of the high heat at which it's cooked. It can be topped with a variety of sweet or savory items, and at Ó, those toppings have Spanish or Asian flair. This is a double-decker variation, which means we use a top and bottom crust.

If you do not wish to make the crust yourself, you may order our ready-made crusts at www.kitchensofbiro.com.

---

2 sheets Tarte Flambée Crust (see page 160)
4 tablespoons Quark Topping (see page 161)
2 ounces mixed greens
8 Roma tomato slices
1 cup grated Manchego cheese
1 cup grated mozzarella cheese
5 ounces Serrano ham, julienned
2 teaspoons Ó SpanAsian Seasoning Mix (see page 158)
Chopped flat-leaf parsley for garnish

---

1 Preheat oven to 450 degrees F.

2 Place a Tarte Flambée Crust on a sheet pan lined with parchment paper.

3 Using a silicone spatula or large spoon, spread the Quark Topping over the crust.

4 Cover evenly with the greens, tomatoes, cheeses, and ham. Sprinkle with the Ó SpanAsian Seasoning Mix.

5 Place the other sheet of Tarte Flambée Crust over the toppings. Bake for 10 minutes, or until the edges are golden brown. Carefully turn over the tarte, and bake for 5 additional minutes, or until the bottom becomes golden brown on the edges. Serve immediately.

[MAKES 1 TARTE]

PRESENTATION

At Ó, we serve this dish traditionally, which is on a wooden board. You could use a large sushi board or even a cutting board, carefully sliding the tarte from the parchment paper, and then slicing it into pieces. Garnish with the parsley. This is a rustic dish, so your guests should feel free to eat it with their hands.

BEVERAGE PAIRINGS

Viña Sila "Naia"
Rueda, Spain

Bodegas González Lara
Fuente del Conde
Rosado de Tempranillo
Cigales, Spain

Quick Tip: What's Quark?

Quark is a soft German cheese with a light, tangy flavor. It's popping up in more and more specialty groceries in the United States, and is widely available online. Click www.germanfoods.org, a fantastic nonprofit site that links Americans to their favorite German products. You could also substitute cream cheese for it in this recipe. You would need to thin the Quark Topping recipe (see page 161) with 2 tablespoons heavy cream and eliminate the crème fraîche. Or you could simply use the crème fraîche on its own, without any cream cheese.

Torta del Casar Cheese & Serrano Ham Tarte Flambée

Torta del Casar cheese is a soft, Spanish ewe's milk cheese. If you're not able to locate it, use Brie or Camembert instead.

---

1 Tarte Flambée Crust (see page 160)
4 tablespoons Quark Topping (see page 161)
5 ounces Serrano ham, julienned
5 ounces Torta del Casar cheese, crumbled
2 teaspoons Ó SpanAsian Seasoning Mix (see page 158)

1 Preheat oven to 450 degrees F.

2 Place the Tarte Flambée Crust on a sheet pan lined with parchment paper.

3 Using a silicone spatula or large spoon, spread the Quark Topping over the crust.

4 Cover evenly with the ham and cheese. Sprinkle with the Ó SpanAsian Seasoning Mix.

5 Bake for 10 minutes, or until the edges are golden brown.

[MAKES 1 TARTE]

PRESENTATION

At Ó, we serve this dish traditionally, which is on a wooden board. You could use a large sushi board or even a cutting board, carefully sliding the tarte from the parchment paper, and then slicing it into pieces. This is a rustic dish, so your guests should feel free to eat it with their hands.

BEVERAGE PAIRINGS

Torres Viña Sol
Penedes, Spain

Damn Bier
Pilsner Lager
Spanish Beer

Spanish Meatball Tarte Flambée with Spicy Tomato Sauce

This tarte's got a bit of kick, but kids love it as much as adults. If you're ambitious, you may wish to make your own meatballs, but frozen ones work great and yield delectable results much quicker!

1 Tarte Flambée Crust (see page 160)
4 tablespoons Quark Topping (see page 161)
2 tablespoons Arrabiata Sauce (see page 159)
20 (½-ounce) frozen meatballs
1½ cups grated mozzarella cheese
½ cup freshly grated Pecorino cheese
2 teaspoons Ó SpanAsian Seasoning Mix (see page 158)

1 Preheat oven to 450 degrees F.

2 Place the Tarte Flambée Crust on a sheet pan lined with parchment paper.

3 Using a silicone spatula or large spoon, spread the Quark Topping over the crust. Spread the Arrabiata Sauce evenly over the Quark Topping.

4 Cover evenly with the meatballs and cheeses. Sprinkle with the Ó SpanAsian Seasoning Mix.

5 Bake for 10 minutes, or until the edges are golden brown.

[MAKES 1 TARTE]

PRESENTATION

At Ó, we serve this dish traditionally, which is on a wooden board. You could use a large sushi board or even a cutting board, carefully sliding the tarte from the parchment paper, and then slicing it into pieces. This is a rustic dish, so your guests should feel free to eat it with their hands.

BEVERAGE PAIRINGS

Olivares Monastrell-Altos de la Hoya
Jumilla, Spain

Castaño
Coleccion
Yecla, Spain

Mushroom, Onion & Cheese Tarte Flambée

You can use the mushroom or mushrooms of your choice for this tarte. We've used anything from simple button mushrooms to morels. For an Asian-inspired flavor, try a blend of shiitake, oyster, and enoki mushrooms.

1 Tarte Flambée Crust (see page 160)
4 tablespoons Quark Topping (see page 161)
1 small yellow onion, diced
½ cup sliced mushrooms
½ cup freshly grated Parmesan cheese
1½ cups grated mozzarella cheese
2 teaspoons Ó SpanAsian Seasoning Mix (see page 158)

1   Preheat oven to 450 degrees F.

2   Place the Tarte Flambée Crust on a sheet pan lined with parchment paper.

3   Using a silicone spatula or large spoon, spread the Quark Topping over the crust.

4   Cover evenly with the onion, mushrooms, and cheeses. Sprinkle with the Ó SpanAsian Seasoning Mix.

5   Bake for 10 minutes, or until the edges are golden brown.

[MAKES 1 TARTE]

PRESENTATION

At Ó, we serve this dish traditionally, which is on a wooden board. You could use a large sushi board or even a cutting board, carefully sliding the tarte from the parchment paper, and then slicing it into pieces. This is a rustic dish, so your guests should feel free to eat it with their hands.

BEVERAGE PAIRINGS

Pazo de Senorans Albariño
Rias Baixas, Spain

Cruz Campo
Pilsner Lager
Spanish Beer

Quick Tip: Making Ó House Crackers

People can't get enough of the seasoned crackers we serve with tapas, and now you can make them at home. Simply place a Tarte Flambée Crust on a sheet pan lined with parchment paper and sprinkle with about 2 teaspoons Ó SpanAsian Seasoning Mix. Bake for 8 minutes, or until the edges are golden brown. Cut or break into pieces before serving. Leftovers can be stored in an airtight container for up to 3 days.

Serrano Ham & Onion Tarte Flambée

This is a Spanish-inspired version of Alsace's most famous tarte flambée, which is covered with quark, bacon, and onions. We use Serrano ham at Ó, but you could use prosciutto, or even applewood-smoked bacon.

1 Tarte Flambée Crust (see page 160)
4 tablespoons Quark Topping (see page 161)
8 ounces Serrano ham, julienned
1 small yellow onion, sliced
½ cup freshly grated Pecorino cheese
1½ cups grated mozzarella cheese
2 teaspoons Ó SpanAsian Seasoning Mix (see page 158)
Chopped flat-leaf parsley for garnish

1   Preheat oven to 450 degrees F.

2   Place the Tarte Flambée Crust on a sheet pan lined with parchment paper.

3   Using a silicone spatula or large spoon, spread the Quark Topping over the crust.

4   Cover evenly with the ham, onion, and cheeses. Sprinkle with the Ó SpanAsian Seasoning Mix.

5   Bake for 10 minutes, or until the edges are golden brown.

[MAKES 1 TARTE]

PRESENTATION

At Ó, we serve this dish traditionally, which is on a wooden board. You could use a large sushi board or even a cutting board, carefully sliding the tarte from the parchment paper, and then slicing it into pieces. Garnish with the parsley. This is a rustic dish, so your guests should feel free to eat it with their hands.

BEVERAGE PAIRINGS

Pazo San Mauro Albariño
Rias Baixas, Spain

Mahou Pilsner Lager
Spain

Quick Tip: What's a Julienne?

You've heard the term julienne throughout this book. What is it? Julienne, also known as an alumette, is a cut in which food is sliced into thin, ⅛-inch-thick matchstick strips between 1 and 2 inches long. Cutting foods into uniform shapes and sizes ensures even cooking and makes for great presentation.

Manchego, Tomato & Spinach Tarte Flambée

This tarte tastes great and has wonderful eye appeal. It's a huge hit at informal cocktails receptions held at the restaurant, and on the regular menu.

1 Tarte Flambée Crust (see page 160)
4 tablespoons Quark Topping (see page 161)
8 slices Roma tomato
1½ cups packed baby spinach leaves, stems removed, julienned
1 cup grated Manchego cheese
1 cup grated mozzarella cheese
2 teaspoons Ó SpanAsian Seasoning Mix (see page 158)

1 Preheat oven to 450 degrees F.

2 Place the Tarte Flambée Crust on a sheet pan lined with parchment paper.

3 Using a silicone spatula or large spoon, spread the Quark Topping over the crust.

4 Cover evenly with the tomato, spinach, and cheeses. Sprinkle with the Ó SpanAsian Seasoning Mix.

5 Bake for 10 minutes, or until the edges are golden brown.

[MAKES 1 TARTE]

PRESENTATION

At Ó, we serve this dish traditionally, which is on a wooden board. You could use a large sushi board or even a cutting board, carefully sliding the tarte from the parchment paper, and then slicing it into pieces. This is a rustic dish, so your guests should feel free to eat it with their hands.

BEVERAGE PAIRINGS

Torres Viña Sol
Penedes, Spain

Capçanes
Mas Donis Barrica
Tarragona, Spain

Quick Tip: Chorizo Variation

Adding chorizo to this tarte gives it a completely different flavor profile. If using Spanish chorizo, you'll get a husky flavor, and if Mexican, a sweetly spiced one. Both are fantastic! Simply crumble 6 ounces chorizo—casings removed—over the Quark Topping in step 3.

Spicy Sesame Shrimp Pasta

This zesty dish has a blend of scallions, ginger, garlic, and Asian spice that clings to perfectly al dente cellentani noodles. Cellentani is a substantial corkscrew-shaped pasta with a tubular center and ridged surface that captures every drop of sauce. The Barilla brand pasta stands up to even the heartiest toppings.

1 (16-ounce) box dried cellentani pasta
½ cup extra virgin olive oil
8 ounces rock shrimp
¼ cup sliced garlic
1 teaspoon Thai chile pepper
¼ cup sliced pickled sushi-style ginger
¼ cup sliced scallions
1 tablespoon soy sauce
¼ cup black sesame seeds
1 tablespoon sesame oil
Sea salt
Freshly ground black pepper
Chopped flat-leaf parsley for garnish

1   Prepare the pasta according to the package instructions.

2   Heat the olive oil in a very large sauté pan over high heat. Add the shrimp and garlic, and sauté for 2 minutes. Add the chile pepper, ginger, and scallions.

3   Deglaze the pan by adding the soy sauce and gently scraping the bits that cling to the bottom of the pan.

4   Add the pasta to heat through; toss well to coat. Add the sesame seeds and sesame oil. Season with salt and pepper.

[SERVES 4]

PRESENTATION

Place in serving dishes and garnish with the parsley. Serve immediately.

BEVERAGE PAIRINGS

Ürziger Würzgarten by A. Merkelbach
Mosel-Saar, Germany

Montsarra
Cava Brut
Catalonia, Spain

Chicken, Pesto & Manchego Tarte Flambée

This tarte is a guest favorite. For variation, you may wish to add crumbled goat cheese.

1 Tarte Flambée Crust (see page 160)
4 tablespoons Quark Topping (see page 161)
½ cup shredded Pesto-Marinated Chicken Breast
   (see page 155)
½ cup grated Parmesan cheese
1½ cups grated mozzarella cheese
2 teaspoons Ó SpanAsian Seasoning Mix (see page 158)

1   Preheat oven to 450 degrees F.

2   Place the Tarte Flambée Crust on a sheet pan lined with parchment paper.

3   Using a silicone spatula or large spoon, spread the Quark Topping over the crust.

4   Cover with the chicken and cheeses. Sprinkle with the Ó SpanAsian Seasoning Mix.

5   Bake for 10 minutes, or until the edges are golden brown.

[MAKES 1 TARTE]

At Ó, we serve this dish traditionally, which is on a wooden board. You could use a large sushi board or even a cutting board, carefully sliding the tarte from the parchment paper, and then slicing it into pieces. This is a rustic dish, so your guests should feel free to eat it with their hands.

BEVERAGE PAIRINGS

Bodegas Nekeas
Vega Sindoa Chardonnay
Navarra, Spain

Bodegas Nekeas
Vega Sindoa "El Chaparral"
Navarra, Spain

Five-Cheese Tarte Flambée

This tarte flambée is covered with quark, Manchego, Parmesan, mozzarella, and Cabrales cheeses that bake up bubbly, golden brown, and delicious. After just one taste, your family will be begging for this ooey, gooey goodness to grace the dinner table every week.

If Cabrales cheese is not available, substitute another Spanish bleu cheese, such as Picos de Europa or Gamonedo, or a French bleu, such as Roquefort.

---

1 Tarte Flambée Crust (see page 160)
4 tablespoons Quark Topping (see page 161)
½ cup grated Manchego cheese
½ cup freshly grated Parmesan cheese
1 cup grated mozzarella cheese
¼ cup crumbled Cabrales cheese
2 teaspoons Ó SpanAsian Seasoning Mix (see page 158)
Chopped flat-leaf parsley for garnish

---

1 Preheat oven to 450 degrees F.

2 Place the Tarte Flambée Crust on a sheet pan lined with parchment paper.

3 Using a silicone spatula or large spoon, spread the Quark Topping over the crust.

4 Cover with the cheeses. Sprinkle with the Ó SpanAsian Seasoning Mix.

5 Bake for 10 minutes, or until the edges are golden brown.

[MAKES 1 TARTE]

PRESENTATION

At Ó, we serve this dish traditionally, which is on a wooden board. You could use a large sushi board or even a cutting board, carefully sliding the tarte from the parchment paper, and then slicing it into pieces. Garnish with the parsley. This is a rustic dish, so your guests should feel free to eat it with their hands.

BEVERAGE PAIRINGS

Viña Sila "Naia"
Rueda, Spain

Con de Albarei
Albariño
Rias Baias, Spain

Spice-Rubbed Steak, Garlic & Onion Tarte Flambée

For carb counters, tarte flambées are a fantastic alternative to pizza, especially when topped with protein-packed steak. Indulge guilt free!

1 teaspoon extra virgin olive oil
3 teaspoons Ó SpanAsian Seasoning Mix (see page 158), divided
4 cloves garlic, minced
1 (4-ounce) hanger steak
1 Tarte Flambée Crust (see page 160)
4 tablespoons Quark Topping (see page 161)
1 small yellow onion, sliced
½ cup freshly grated pecorino cheese
1½ cups grated mozzarella cheese
1 tablespoon chopped cilantro for garnish

1   Preheat oven to 450 degrees F.

2   Heat a grill or grill pan to high heat.

3   Combine the oil, 1 teaspoon Ó SpanAsian Seasoning Mix, and the garlic in a small bowl. Rub this mixture into the steak. Grill until medium-rare, about 1½ minutes on each side. Thinly slice.

4   Place the Tarte Flambée Crust on a sheet pan lined with parchment paper.

5   Using a silicone spatula or large spoon, spread the Quark Topping over the crust.

6   Cover evenly with the steak, onion, and cheeses. Sprinkle with the remaining Ó SpanAsian Seasoning Mix.

7   Bake for 10 minutes, or until the edges are golden brown.

[MAKES 1 TARTE]

PRESENTATION

At Ó, we serve this dish traditionally, which is on a wooden board. You could use a large sushi board or even a cutting board, carefully sliding the tarte from the parchment paper, and then slicing it into pieces. Garnish with the cilantro. This is a rustic dish, so your guests should feel free to eat it with their hands.

BEVERAGE PAIRINGS

Viña Mayor
Reserve
Ribera del Duero, Spain

Agricola Falset Marca
Etim
Tarragona, Spain

Spicy Calamari, Shrimp, Garlic, Tomato, Spinach & Mushroom Tarte Flambée

This tarte is a seafood lover's dream. Serve it with the Spice-Rubbed Steak, Garlic & Onion Tarte Flambée on page 61, and you've got the ultimate surf and turf combination.

---

1 Tarte Flambée Crust (see page 160)
4 tablespoons Quark Topping (see page 161)
8 slices Roma tomato
1½ cups packed baby spinach leaves, stems removed, julienned
¾ cup thinly sliced mushrooms
2 tablespoons extra virgin olive oil
3 cloves garlic, minced
1 ounce rock shrimp
1 ounce baby calamari
½ cup freshly grated pecorino cheese
1½ cups grated mozzarella cheese
2 teaspoons Ó SpanAsian Seasoning Mix (see page 158)
Chopped flat-leaf parsley for garnish

1 Preheat oven to 450 degrees F.

2 Place the Tarte Flambée Crust on a sheet pan lined with parchment paper.

3 Using a silicone spatula or large spoon, spread the Quark Topping over the crust.

4 Cover evenly with the tomato, spinach, and mushrooms.

5 Heat the oil in a large sauté pan over high heat. Add the garlic, shrimp, and calamari, and sauté for 2 minutes. Spoon evenly over the tarte. Top with the cheeses.

Sprinkle with the Ó SpanAsian Seasoning Mix.

6 Bake for 10 minutes, or until the edges are golden brown.

[MAKES 1 TARTE]

PRESENTATION

At Ó, we serve this dish traditionally, which is on a wooden board. You could use a large sushi board or even a cutting board, carefully sliding the tarte from the parchment paper, and then slicing it into pieces. Garnish with the parsley. This is a rustic dish, so your guests should feel free to eat it with their hands.

BEVERAGE PAIRINGS

Caceres Satinela
Rioja, Spain

Albet I Noya
Chardonnay Blend
Penedés, Spain

Sushi&Tapas

Birómaki

This is our version of the California roll. Instead of imitation crab, we use peekytoe crab. We also use tobiko, which adds color and flavor, and Japanese Mayonnaise, which adds zest.

Like the California roll, the Birómaki is an inside-out roll, which means the nori is on the inside, and the rice is on the outside.

½ **recipe Sushi Rice (see page 161)**
3 half sheets nori, dampened with water
1 small cucumber, peeled and seeded
1 small avocado
2 tablespoons Japanese Mayonnaise (see page 161),
    plus more for dipping
⅛ **teaspoon wasabi paste, plus more for dipping**
5 ounces peekytoe crabmeat
2 tablespoons tobiko
Sliced pickled sushi-style ginger for garnish
Soy sauce for dipping

1   Place a bamboo mat down so that the grain is horizontal. Cover with plastic wrap. Dip your hands in warm water to prevent the rice from sticking to them, and spread a bit of water and one-third of the rice over the plastic wrap so that it is the same size as the nori sheets. Place a sheet of nori shiny side down on the rice.

2   Cut the cucumber into strips the same length as the nori sheets. Cut the avocado into juliennes.

3   Spread a tiny amount of Japanese Mayonnaise down the center of the nori. Cover with one-third of the wasabi paste, the cucumber, avocado, and crabmeat. Lift the closest end of the bamboo mat up over the filling. Press the roll firmly inside the bamboo mat, and continue rolling. Transfer the roll to a platter, and remove the bamboo mat. Repeat with the remaining nori. Roll in the tobiko and slice each roll into 8 pieces.

[SERVES 4]

PRESENTATION

Arrange the rolls on a wooden board. Garnish with the ginger, and serve with the Japanese Mayonnaise, the remaining wasabi paste, and soy sauce for dipping. Serve immediately, and discard any leftovers.

BEVERAGE PAIRINGS

Fukumasamune Sake
Ishikawa, Japan

Reuscher Haart
Piesporter Goldtropfehen
Riesling Kabinett
Mosel, Germany

Nori Rolls

These small, easy-to-make sushi rolls come in four variations: tuna, salmon, wasabi, and cucumber. We serve them with wasabi, Japanese Mayonnaise, and soy sauce for dipping.

Daikon is a large Asian radish that's sweet and has a bit of bite. It's great used raw in salads, sautéed in stir-fry, and shredded as a garnish.

---

4 ounces sushi-grade tuna

⅛ cup sake

⅛ cup soy sauce

2 recipes Sushi Rice (see page 161)

8 half sheets nori, dampened with water

1 tablespoon wasabi paste

4 ounces salmon filet

½ teaspoon sesame oil

4 ounces marinated daikon

1 small cucumber, peeled and seeded

2 tablespoons Japanese Mayonnaise (see page 161), plus more for dipping

Sliced pickled sushi-style ginger for garnish

Wasabi paste for dipping

Soy sauce for dipping

1 To make the tuna rolls, cut the tuna into 2-ounce strips the same length as the nori sheets.

2 Bring the sake to a boil in a small saucepan over high heat. Remove from heat, and allow to cool. Stir in the soy sauce.

3 Marinate the tuna in the sake-soy sauce blend for 2 minutes.

4 Place a bamboo mat down so that the grain is horizontal. Place a sheet of nori shiny side down on the mat. Dip your hands in warm water to prevent the rice from sticking to them, and spread one-eighth of the rice over the nori, leaving a ½-inch border on the long side opposite you.

5 Spread a tiny amount of wasabi down the center of the rice. Cover with half of the tuna. Lift the closest end of the bamboo mat up over the tuna. Press the roll firmly inside the bamboo mat, and continue rolling. Transfer the roll to a platter, and remove the bamboo mat. Repeat with the remaining tuna.

6 To make the salmon rolls, cut the salmon into 2-ounce strips the same length as the nori sheets.

7 Spread a tiny amount of the oil on the top of each salmon strip.

8 Place a bamboo mat down so that the grain is horizontal. Place a sheet of nori shiny side down on the mat. Dip your hands in warm water to prevent the rice from sticking to them, and spread a bit of water and one-eighth of the rice over the nori, leaving a ½-inch border on the long side opposite you.

9 Place half of the salmon down the center of the rice. Lift the closest end of the bamboo mat up over the

continued on page 70

salmon. Press the roll firmly inside the bamboo mat, and continue rolling. Transfer the roll to a platter, and remove the bamboo mat. Repeat with the remaining salmon.

10 To make the wasabi rolls, cut the daikon into 2-ounce strips the same length as the nori sheets.

11 Place a bamboo mat down so that the grain is horizontal. Place a sheet of nori, shiny side down, on the mat. Dip your hands in warm water to prevent the rice from sticking to them, and spread one-eighth of the rice over the nori, leaving a ½-inch border on the long side opposite you.

12 Spread a tiny amount of wasabi down the center of the rice. Cover with half of the daikon. Lift the closest end of the bamboo mat up over the daikon. Press the roll firmly inside the bamboo mat, and continue rolling. Transfer the roll to a platter and remove the bamboo mat. Repeat with the remaining daikon.

13 To make the cucumber rolls, cut the cucumber into strips the same length as the nori sheets.

14 Place a bamboo mat down so that the grain is horizontal. Place a sheet of nori, shiny side down, on the mat. Dip your hands in warm water to prevent the rice from sticking to them, and spread a bit of water and one-eighth of the rice over the nori, leaving a ½-inch border on the long side opposite you.

15 Spread a tiny amount of Japanese Mayonnaise down the center of the rice. Cover with half of the cucumber. Lift the closest end of the bamboo mat up over the cucumber. Press the roll firmly inside the bamboo mat, and continue rolling. Transfer the roll to a platter, and remove the bamboo mat. Repeat with the remaining cucumber.

[SERVES 4]

PRESENTATION

Slice the rolls, and place on a wooden board. Garnish with the ginger, and serve with the wasabi paste, Japanese Mayonnaise, and soy sauce for dipping. Serve immediately, and discard any leftovers.

BEVERAGE PAIRINGS

Fukumasamune Sake
Ishikawa, Japan

Reuscher Haart
Piesporter Goldtropfehen
Riesling Kabinett
Mosel, Germany

Nigiri-Zushi

The type of sushi most commonly found in sushi bars, nigiri-zushi derives its name from the Japanese word *nigiri*, which means squeeze. While some people create it by gently squeezing together bite-sized slices of fish with small balls of rice, body heat can make sushi rice sticky. Instead, we use two spoons to form quenelles, or egg shapes, of rice, and then cover them with fish. You can also purchase forms to shape the rice.

---

2 recipes Sushi Rice (see page 161)
4 ounces tuna
4 ounces salmon
4 ounces whitefish
2 tablespoons wasabi paste, plus more for dipping
4 prawns
Sliced pickled sushi-style ginger for garnish
Soy sauce for dipping

1   Using two teaspoons that have been dipped in hot water, form the rice into egg shapes by using one teaspoon to hold the rice, and the other to shape it.

2   Bring a small pot of salted water to a boil.

3   Meanwhile, line a sheet pan with plastic wrap. Slice the tuna, salmon, and whitefish into thin pieces that will cover the tops of the molded rice. Place the slices on the sheet pan. Spread a tiny amount of wasabi paste onto each slice.

4   Wash the prawns under cool running water, and cut off the heads.

5   Insert a bamboo skewer through the prawns from head to tail; drop the prawns into the boiling salt water. When the prawns change color and rise to the top, they're done, 3 to 5 minutes. Plunge the prawns into an ice bath; when cooled, drain. Remove the skewer by using a screwing motion.

6   Remove the shells from around the body, but not the tails. Lay the prawns down with the tails away from you. Cut from the heads to the tails, along the belly, cutting halfway through the flesh. Using your fingers, open up and flatten the prawns, being careful not to damage the flesh. Using the tip of a sharp knife, remove the vein and rinse the prawns under cool, running water.

7   Spread a tiny amount of wasabi onto the undersides of the prawns.

8   Cover each ball of rice with a slice of fish or a prawn, wasabi side down.

[S E R V E S   8]

P R E S E N T A T I O N

Serve on a wooden board garnished with pickled sushi-style ginger, wasabi paste, and soy sauce. Serve immediately, and discard any leftovers. Nigiri-Zushi is great served with a selection of dipping sauces (see next page).

B E V E R A G E   P A I R I N G S

Fukumasamune Sake
Ishikawa, Japan

Reuscher Haart
Piesporter Goldtropfehen
Riesling Kabinett
Mosel, Germany

Sushi Dipping Sauces

Dipping sauces are a great addition to any type of sushi. Here are a few that are easy to make and are great served with Nigiri-Zushi:

SWEET SAUCE

⅓ **cup ketchup**
3 **tablespoons honey**
3 **tablespoons pineapple juice**
1 **tablespoon soy sauce**
3 **tablespoons vegetable oil**

Combine the ketchup and honey in a small bowl. Pour in the juice and soy sauce, and mix well to combine. Add the oil in a slow, steady stream, and whisk to emulsify.

YELLOW SAUCE

2 **egg yolks**
2 **tablespoons rice wine vinegar**
1 **tablespoon sugar**
2 **tablespoons dashi***
Karashi mustard

This sauce uses karashi mustard, which is Japanese mustard flavored with horseradish. You can find it in Asian markets.

Whisk together the yolks, vinegar, sugar, and dashi in a small bowl. Add the mustard to taste.

*Dashi is a flavorful vegetarian soup stock widely used in Japan. To make it, soak a 6-inch piece of kombu, or dried kelp, in 4 cups water for 1 hour. Bring the water and kombu to a boil in a medium saucepan over low heat.

GINGER DIPPING SAUCE

⅓ **cup soy sauce**
⅓ **cup sake**
2 **tablespoons sugar**
1 **teaspoon minced garlic**
1 **teaspoon grated ginger**
2 **tablespoons vegetable oil**

Whisk together the soy sauce, sake, sugar, garlic, and ginger in a small bowl. Add the oil in a slow, steady stream, and whisk to emulsify.

Sushi Tools

Many people assume that to make sushi, they need a lot of special tools and equipment. Not true. In fact, there are only a few items we suggest having on hand to make sushi.

RICE COOKER

A rice cooker is a good investment. It will keep your rice at the perfect temperature and will produce rice of a consistent quality.

QUALITY CHEF'S KNIFE

A good, sharp chef's knife is key. It will enable you to slice your fish paper thin and will also ensure nice, even cuts when slicing sushi rolls.

BAMBOO MAT

Bamboo mats are flexible and nonstick. They'll help you roll your sushi tightly and effortlessly.

BAMBOO SPOON

A bamboo spoon is a very inexpensive investment that will make your job a lot easier. Rice doesn't stick to it, so when seasoning your rice for sushi, the grains stay where they are supposed to.

PAPER FAN

Marcel jokes that a cheap paper fan serves two purposes: it enables you to quickly cool your rice to a lukewarm temperature suitable for handling, and it's also good for cooling the chef when the kitchen gets too hot.

Just remember, when making sushi, nothing is as important to your sushi as fresh ingredients.

Ó Olive Spread

This is a fantastic tapa to serve with bread, crackers, and wine at an informal gathering. You could also slather it atop a rustic sandwich or over grilled fish.

You may wish to use chopped flat-leaf parsley, cilantro, or chives—or a combination of the three—for the garnish.

---

1 cup cured black olives, pitted
1 cup cured green olives, pitted
1 can anchovies, drained
2 Roma tomatoes, sliced
1 small yellow onion, chopped
4 cloves garlic
½ tablespoon capers
¾ cup freshly grated Parmesan cheese
1 cup extra virgin olive oil
1 baguette, cut into ½-inch-thick slices, toasted
Minced herbs for garnish

———

1   Place the olives, anchovies, tomatoes, onion, garlic, capers, and cheese in a food processor, and pulse.

2   Add the oil in a slow, steady stream to emulsify. Pulse until the mixture still has small chunks but is fine enough to spread.

[SERVES 4 TO 6]

PRESENTATION

Spread over the toasted bread slices, and garnish with the herbs. You may wish to add a drizzle of olive oil.

BEVERAGE PAIRINGS

Adegas Morgadio
Morgadio Albariño
Rais Baixas, Spain

Pasanau
Finca la Planeta
Priorato, Spain

Japanese Barbecue Chicken Skewers

The Japanese take their barbecued chicken seriously; in fact, they have entire restaurants that serve only barbecued chicken, sake, and beer. This dish—made with sake, mirin, soy sauce, and shichimi togarashi—give the skewers authentic Japanese flavor. Shichimi togarashi is a blend of seven spices, including bell pepper, that is used widely in Japanese cooking. If it's not available, substitute sansho, or Japanese pepper. Both are available in Asian markets. You could also use our Ó SpanAsian Seasoning Mix (see page 158).

Soak the bamboo skewers in water for a minimum of 10 minutes before using, to prevent the wood from burning.

½ **cup sake**
½ **cup mirin**
2 tablespoons sugar
½ **cup soy sauce**
7 ounces chicken breast, cut into 1-inch cubes
7 ounces chicken thigh, cut into 1-inch cubes
½ **leek, cut into 1-inch pieces**
Shichimi togarashi

━━━━━━━━━━

1 Preheat a grill or grill pan.

2 Combine the sake, mirin, sugar, and soy sauce in a small saucepan over high heat, and bring to a boil. Reduce by two-thirds.

3 Thread the chicken cubes and leek pieces in alternating order on the skewers. Grill until golden brown on all sides, frequently brushing with the marinade.

[SERVES 4]

PRESENTATION

Sprinkle with shichimi togarashi, and serve family style.

BEVERAGE PAIRINGS

Bodegas Muga
Rioja Rosado
Rioja, Spain

Bodegas Agapito Rico
Carchelo Monastrell
Jumilla, Spain

Roasted Artichokes with Garlic, Sun-Dried Tomatoes & Goat Cheese

This tapa is simply heavenly. If you toss the dish with pasta, it becomes an entrée. Either way, Roasted Artichokes with Garlic, Sun-Dried Tomatoes & Goat Cheese is sure to become one of your favorite recipes.

If you don't wish to trim the artichokes yourself, use high-quality, unmarinated canned artichokes.

---

6 medium artichokes
⅓ cup lemon juice
⅔ cup extra virgin olive oil
1 large head garlic, peeled
½ cup julienned sun-dried tomatoes
1 teaspoon minced thyme
1 Turkish bay leaf
Sea salt
Freshly ground black pepper
10 ounces goat cheese

1 Preheat oven to 325 degrees F.

2 Bend the tough outer leaves of the first artichoke backward until they break at the point where the tough leaf meets the tender base. Stop when you reach the more tender yellow-green interior leaves. With a serrated knife, cut across the top of the artichoke where the color changes from yellow-green to dark green. Trim the base, removing any discolorations. Halve the artichoke lengthwise, and scoop out the hairy choke with a spoon. Repeat with the remaining artichokes.

3 Place the trimmed artichokes into a large, non-reactive bowl a couple at a time, and drizzle with the lemon juice to prevent oxidation, tossing them in the bowl so that they are completely coated in lemon juice.

4 Place the artichokes and juice in a roasting pan over medium heat. Add the oil, garlic, sun-dried tomatoes, thyme, and bay leaf. Season with salt and pepper. Bring to a boil, stirring occasionally.

5 Transfer to the oven and bake for 35 minutes, or until the artichokes are browned in spots and tender when pierced. Allow to cool slightly, and then cut each artichoke lengthwise into quarters.

[SERVES 6]

PRESENTATION

Heat the broiler. Drizzle the tapa with the infused oil from the bottom of the pan. Crumble the goat cheese over the top. Broil for 1 minute, or until the cheese is browned. Serve family style with crusty bread.

BEVERAGE PAIRINGS

Artadi
Crianza Viñas de Gain
Rioja, Spain

Huguet
Can Feixes Blanc Selecció
Cataluna, Spain

Lamb Cracklings with Cabrales Cheese & Honey

Cracklings are crunchy pieces of meat that have been rendered, or cooked until the connective tissue separates and becomes crispy. Here, we dip lamb cracklings in our Velouté, and then bread and fry them until golden brown. We serve them with honey for dipping.

---

1 (3-pound) leg of lamb, de-boned
1 cup Velouté (see page 155)
7 ounces crumbled Cabrales cheese
2 tablespoons minced cilantro, divided
Sea salt
Freshly ground black pepper
Vegetable oil for frying
½ cup flour
2 large eggs
1 teaspoon heavy cream
1 cup breadcrumbs
Honey for dipping

1 Preheat oven to 350 degrees F.

2 Place the lamb in a shallow baking dish, and roast for 15 minutes, rotating every 5 minutes so each side cooks evenly.

3 Remove from the oven, and allow to cool.

4 Place the Velouté in a saucepan and warm, stirring frequently, over medium-high heat. Add the cheese, and stir until melted. Add half of the cilantro, and season with salt and pepper.

5 Cut the lamb into ½-inch-thick slices. Dip into the Velouté-cheese mixture. Place on a sheet pan lined with Silpat, and refrigerate for about 10 minutes, or until chilled.

6 Heat the oil to 375 degrees F.

7 Remove the lamb from the refrigerator. Place the flour in a shallow dish. Whisk together the eggs and cream in a second shallow dish to make an egg wash. Place the breadcrumbs in a third shallow dish. Dredge the chilled lamb in the flour, tapping gently to remove excess. Place them in the egg wash and cover completely, and then remove and shake gently to remove excess. Place the eggwashed lamb into the breadcrumbs, and coat completely.

8 Fry the lamb in the oil until crispy and golden brown, about 3 minutes. Drain on paper towels.

[SERVES 6]

PRESENTATION

You may wish to serve Lamb Cracklings "pub style," in a parchment paper or newspaper cone that you can fashion yourself with just a piece of tape. Sprinkle with the remaining cilantro, and serve with the honey for dipping.

BEVERAGE PAIRINGS

Jaume Serra
Tinto Reserva
Penedes, Spain

Vall Llach
Embruix
Priorato, Spain

Marinated Olives & Cheese with Spice-Sautéed Almonds

Here, olives and cheese each get their own flavor-packed marinades, and almonds are sautéed with a bit of spice. Serve at your next gathering, or place in separate glass jars to give as a unique hostess gift.

MARINATED OLIVES

½ teaspoon coriander seeds
½ teaspoon fennel seeds
1 teaspoon chopped rosemary
2 tablespoons chopped parsley
2 cloves garlic, minced
⅔ cup cured black olives
⅔ cup cured green olives
1 tablespoon sherry vinegar
2 tablespoons extra virgin olive oil

MARINATED CHEESE

5 ounces Manchego cheese, cut into ½-inch cubes
6 tablespoons extra virgin olive oil
1 teaspoon black peppercorns
1 clove garlic, sliced
2 sprigs thyme, chopped
2 sprigs tarragon, chopped
1 tablespoon chopped parsley

SPICE-SAUTÉED ALMONDS

4 tablespoons unsalted butter
4 tablespoons extra virgin olive oil
1¾ cups blanched almonds
¼ teaspoon cayenne pepper
½ tablespoon sea salt

FOR THE MARINATED OLIVES

Combine all ingredients in a medium bowl, and allow to marinate at room temperature for at least 2 hours.

FOR THE MARINATED CHEESE

Combine all ingredients in a medium bowl, and allow to marinate at room temperature for at least 2 hours.

FOR THE SPICE-SAUTÉED ALMONDS

1 Melt the butter and oil in a large sauté pan over medium-high heat.

2 When the butter oil mixture becomes frothy, add the almonds. Season with the cayenne pepper and salt, and sauté until the almonds are golden brown, about 3 minutes.

[SERVES 6 TO 8]

PRESENTATION

Serve in tiny dishes, a 3-compartment dish, or in an olive tray. They are a great accompaniment to our Ó House Crackers (see page 54).

BEVERAGE PAIRINGS

Alvear Fino (Sherry)
Montilla, Spain

Vinicola del Priorat
Onix
Priorato, Spain

Spanish Beef Strips

This is an easy tapa that, when served over rice or pasta, makes a great main course.

---

1 pound beef tenderloin, cut into 2-inch-long strips
Sea salt
Freshly ground black pepper
1 tablespoon extra virgin olive oil
1 medium yellow onion, sliced
1½ cups button mushrooms, sliced
1 teaspoon smoked pimentón
½ cup dry white wine

1 Pat the beef strips dry with paper towels. Season with salt and pepper.

2 Heat the oil in a large sauté pan over high heat. Add the beef strips, and sauté for 30 seconds. Add the onion and mushrooms, and sauté until golden brown. Sprinkle with the pimentón.

3 Deglaze the pan by adding the wine and gently scraping the bits that cling to the bottom of the pan. Simmer until most of the liquid has evaporated. Season with salt and pepper.

[SERVES 4 TO 6]

PRESENTATION

We like to serve Spanish Beef Strips with our Santa Fe Corn (see page 90) or Creamed Artichokes (see page 89).

BEVERAGE PAIRINGS

Telmo Rodriguez "LZ"
Rioja, Spain

Hacienda Monasterio
Crianza
Ribera del Duero, Spain

Frijoles Cubanos

This is Ó's tapas chef Raul Morales's famous Cuban black bean recipe, which is great served with eggs in the morning, or as an accompaniment to our Trio of Empanadas (see page 86). Some people like to eat them cold.

1 teaspoon extra virgin olive oil
1 ounce Canadian bacon, chopped
1 medium yellow onion, chopped
2 cloves garlic, chopped
2 tablespoons chopped cilantro, plus more for garnish
½ teaspoon cumin
½ teaspoon dried oregano
2 (15-ounce) cans black beans, drained and rinsed
1½ cups Chicken Stock (see page 152)
¼ cup fruity white wine
½ teaspoon sugar

1   Heat the oil in a large sauté pan over high heat. Add the bacon, onion, garlic, cilantro, cumin, and oregano, and sauté until the onion begins to caramelize, about 5 minutes.

2   Add the beans and stock, and simmer for 5 minutes. Add the wine and sugar, and cook for 5 additional minutes.

[SERVES 6 TO 8]

PRESENTATION

Garnish with the cilantro, and serve family style. Frijoles Cubanos are also great served topped with grated Manchego cheese, diced tomatoes, and sliced black olives.

BEVERAGE PAIRINGS

Pucho Mencia
Bierzo, Spain

Bodegas Sierra Cantabria
Rioja Criánza
Rioja, Spain

Santa Fe Corn

Remember your mother's creamed corn? This ain't it! Here, we sauté onions, and then add canned corn, sour cream, and red pepper flakes. The result is a sweet, creamy dish with a bit of bite. For added freshness, use fresh corn when it's in season.

8 tablespoons unsalted butter
1 large yellow onion, thinly sliced
2 (15-ounce) cans sweet corn, drained
1 cup sour cream
2 teaspoons red pepper flakes
Sea salt
Freshly ground black pepper
Ó SpanAsian Seasoning Mix (see page 158)
Chopped flat-leaf parsley for garnish

BEVERAGE PAIRINGS

Sierra Cantabria
Blanco
Rioja, Spain

Vol Damm
Pilsner Lager
Spain

1 Melt the butter in a large sauté pan over high heat. Add the onion, and lightly caramelize, 5 minutes.

2 Add the corn, and sauté for 3 minutes. Stir in the sour cream and red pepper flakes, and sauté for 1 additional minute. Season with salt and pepper.

[SERVES 4 TO 6]

PRESENTATION

Sprinkle with the Ó SpanAsian Seasoning Mix and parsley. Serve with Ó House Crackers (see page 54) or tortilla chips.

What's Caramelization?

Caramelizing means to sauté an onion until its liquid evaporates and its natural sugars are released. Onions with high sugar content, such as Vidalia onions, caramelize faster than those with lower sugar contents, such as white onions.

Teriyaki-Glazed Mushrooms with Sesame

Another simple and flavor-packed tapa that also works well as a side dish, Teriyaki-Glazed Mushrooms with Sesame has a delectable sweet-and-sour flavor that's an excellent accompaniment to our Pork, Steak & Salmon Satay (see page 103).

For a sweeter flavor, you may wish to add 1 tablespoon orange juice with the teriyaki sauce.

---

2 tablespoons extra virgin olive oil
2 cloves garlic, sliced
8 ounces button mushrooms
1 cup teriyaki sauce
Freshly ground black pepper
1 tablespoon toasted white sesame seeds
Cilantro sprigs for garnish

1   Heat the oil in a large sauté pan over high heat. Add the garlic, and sauté for 1 minute. Reduce heat to medium, and add the mushrooms. Sauté until golden brown, about 5 minutes.

2   Add the teriyaki sauce, and simmer for 3 minutes. Season with black pepper, and sprinkle with the sesame seeds.

[S E R V E S   6]

PRESENTATION

Serve in a rustic dish, garnished with the cilantro. Teriyaki-Glazed Mushrooms with Sesame is great served over steak, or on toasted slices of baguette.

BEVERAGE PAIRINGS

Sapporo Premium Beer
Sapporo, Japan

Urakasumi Sake
Miyagi, Japan

Asian Eggplant with Napa Cabbage

This delicious dish adds color and a sweet touch to our tapas bar. We usually use Japanese eggplants for the recipe, as they have thin skins and sweet, delicate flavor. Chinese eggplants will give this dish a more bitter flavor, while using a small Italian eggplant would yield a milder taste.

1 cup extra virgin olive oil
2 Japanese eggplants, chopped
1 Napa cabbage, julienned
½ cup teriyaki sauce
Sea salt
Freshly ground black pepper

1 Heat the oil in a large sauté pan over high heat. Add the eggplant and cabbage, and sauté until the eggplant is golden brown.

2 Deglaze the pan by adding the teriyaki sauce and gently scraping the bits that cling to the bottom of the pan. Simmer until the liquid reduces, about 1 minute. Season with salt and pepper.

[SERVES 4 TO 6]

PRESENTATION

Because of its beautiful color, this tapa should be served in simple white dishes.

For a lovely and delicious presentation, serve it with our Santa Fe Corn (see page 90) and Spanish Beef Strips (see page 84).

BEVERAGE PAIRINGS

Kamotsuru Sake
Hiroshima, Japan

Hakkaizan Sake
Niigata, Japan

Chipotle Pork with Mushrooms

Popular in both Spanish and Asian cuisines, pork is versatile and thus makes a fantastic foundation for a wide array of Ó's tapas. Here, we spice it up with chipotle chiles.

In recent years, chipotles have been popping up on all sorts of menus. It's a chile of medium heat and smoky flavor, and is most commonly used in adobo sauce.

Button mushrooms or baby portabellas work well for this recipe.

---

4 tablespoons extra virgin olive oil, divided
8 ounces pork loin, cubed
2 dried chipotle chiles, crushed
2 tablespoons water
2 medium yellow onions, sliced
8 ounces mushrooms, sliced
Sea salt
Freshly ground black pepper

━━━━━━━━━━

1   Heat 3 tablespoons oil in a medium sauté pan over high heat. Add the pork, and sauté until browned on all sides. Remove the pork from the pan with a slotted spoon, keeping the drippings in the pan.

2   In the same pan in which you sautéed the pork, combine the crushed chiles with the water. Stir over high heat to create a paste.

3   Add the remaining oil, onions, and mushrooms and sauté until the onions are translucent, about 5 minutes.

4   Add the pork cubes back to the pan, and toss to coat and warm through. Season with salt and pepper.

[SERVES 6 TO 8]

PRESENTATION

Serve alone with crusty bread or over rice.

BEVERAGE PAIRINGS

Bodegas Jalon
Albariño
Calatayud, Spain

Alvaro Palacios
Les Terrases
Priorato, Spain

━━━━━━━━━━

Quick Tip: The Fool-Proof Way to Crush Chiles

Crushing hot chiles by hand can be a daunting project for those sensitive to heat. Try using a clean coffee grinder to safely pulverize chiles to a powder consistency.

Sweet-Spiced Pork Ribs

We use pork in a variety of sweeter applications at both our Ó and Biró restaurant concepts: with black cherry-pepper sauce, with apricots, and here, with oloroso sherry, brown sugar, and orange juice.

You can cut the ribs yourself, using a meat cleaver or boning knife, or you can have your butcher do it for you. You'll need a grill or grill pan for this recipe.

1½ pounds pork ribs
6 tablespoons oloroso sherry
1 tablespoon tomato paste
1 teaspoon soy sauce
½ teaspoon Tabasco sauce
1 tablespoon light brown sugar
½ cup orange juice
1 teaspoon sea salt
2 tablespoons flour

---

1   Heat a grill or grill pan.

2   Separate the ribs with a cleaver, and then cut each rib in half.

3   To make the sauce, in a medium bowl, combine the sherry, tomato paste, soy sauce, Tabasco sauce, brown sugar, and orange juice.

4   Combine the salt and flour in a large, resealable plastic bag. Add the ribs, and shake to coat. Remove the ribs from the bag, and tap gently to remove excess flour.

5   Dredge the ribs in the sauce. Grill, turning occasionally, until tender, about 25 minutes.

[S E R V E S   6   T O   8]

PRESENTATION

You may wish to serve this tapa garnished with a sprig of cilantro and a lime wedge.

BEVERAGE PAIRINGS

Finca Luzon
Verde
Jumilla, Spain

Bodegas Muga
Torre
Rioja, Spain

What's Oloroso Sherry?

Sherry is a fortified Spanish wine sold in two varieties: fino and oloroso. Fino, also sometimes called Palma sherry, is dry and fruity. Examples are the premium varieties of Manzanilla and Amontillado. Oloroso sherry is more heavily fortified, with Amoroso and cream sherry being the two most popular examples. Because it's less expensive than fino sherry, oloroso is the kind most often used in cooking. Sherries labeled as cooking sherry have a high sodium content. Shy away from these.

If sherry is not available, you may use Port or Madeira in this recipe.

Moros y Cristianos

This is our take on the traditional Moros y Cristianos, or Moors and Christians, a Spanish black bean and rice dish that refers to the Moors' invasion of Spain. It is made with Sofrito, a Spanish sauce made by sautéing annatto seeds, pimento, onions, and garlic in rendered pork fat.

BEANS

1 cup black beans
1 small yellow onion, quartered
2 cloves garlic, crushed
1 Turkish bay leaf
¼ cup green pimento
½ teaspoon cumin
½ teaspoon oregano

SOFRITO

1 tablespoon extra virgin olive oil
1 ounce Canadian bacon, cut into strips
½ teaspoon annatto seeds
¼ cup diced yellow onion
¼ cup green pimento, cut into strips
1 clove garlic, minced
2 tablespoons dry white wine
1 teaspoon vinegar
1 teaspoon sugar
Sea salt
Freshly ground black pepper

DISH

2 cups steamed rice

FOR THE BEANS

1   Place all ingredients in a medium pot. Cover with 4 cups water, and bring to a simmer over medium heat. Simmer until the beans are soft, about 45 minutes.

2   Strain, and remove the onion and bay leaf.

FOR THE SOFRITO

1   Heat the oil in a large sauté pan over medium heat. Add the bacon, and sauté until golden brown. Add the annatto seeds, and sauté for 1 minute. Carefully remove the seeds, and then add the onion, pimento, and garlic. Sauté until the onions are glossy.

2   Add the strained beans, and warm through. Deglaze the pan by adding wine and gently scraping the bits that cling to the bottom of the pan. Add the vinegar and sugar, and simmer for 15 minutes.

3   Season with salt and pepper.

[SERVES 6 TO 8]

PRESENTATION

Place the rice in a rustic dish, and top with the beans. Serve immediately.

BEVERAGE PAIRINGS

Dominio de Egurin
Protocolo Tinto
Rioja, Spain

Bodegas Campante
Gran Reboreda
Ribeiro, Spain

Lamb & Garbanzo Bean Ragoût

This tapa makes a delectable main course when served over rice or pasta. You could also serve it on crostini (toasted bread) or as an hors d'oeuvre.

---

5 cups Chicken, Beef, or Vegetable Stock (see pages 152 and 153)
2½ cups garbanzo beans
2 tablespoons extra virgin olive oil
1 large yellow onion, coarsely chopped
½ pound ground lamb
1 tablespoon tomato paste
1 teaspoon sweet pimentón
2 cloves garlic, minced
4 ounces canned green pimentos, drained and chopped
Sea salt
Freshly ground black pepper

1 Bring the stock to a boil. Pour over the beans, and allow to sit for 1 hour.

2 Heat the oil in a large sauté pan over medium heat. Add the onion, and sauté until glossy.

3 Add the lamb, tomato paste, and pimentón, and sauté for 7 minutes. Add the garlic, and sauté for 3 additional minutes.

4 Pour in the beans and stock. Add the pimentos, and simmer for 15 minutes. Season with salt and pepper.

[SERVES 4 TO 6]

PRESENTATION

Serve in a simple white dish. You may wish to add a few sprigs of cilantro for garnish.

BEVERAGE PAIRINGS

Bodegas Borsao
Tres Picos
Borja, Spain

Finca Villa Creces
Crianza
Ribera del Duero, Spain

Main Courses

Pork, Steak & Salmon Satay with Mushrooms, Roasted Bell Peppers,
  Onions & Mixed Greens Salad
Salmon Teriyaki Satay with Garlic-Fried Rice & Mixed Greens Salad
Spice-Grilled Ahi Tuna with Garlic-Fried Rice, Mixed Greens Salad &
  Orange-Sherry Vinaigrette
Grilled Andalusian Spice-Rubbed Steak with Sautéed Shrimp & Spanish
  Potatoes
Asian Salmon Steak with Mushrooms, Mixed Greens Salad & Garlic-
  Fried Rice
Horseradish- & Wasabi-Crusted Sirloin with Rioja & Scalloped Potatoes
Basque Pork Satay with Mixed Greens Salad, Spanish Potatoes & Salted
  Cucumbers
Grilled Hake with Three Spanish Sauces
Sautéed Sea Bass Filets with Orange Sauce, Cauliflower Purée &
  Wasabi Tobiko
Steamed Turbot in Sake Sauce with Fried Citrus Zest & Jasmine Rice
Chorizo-Studded Pork Loin with White Wine & Morcilla Mashed
  Potatoes
Vegetarian Paella
Shredded Chicken Lettuce Wraps
Vegetarian Lettuce Wraps
Flash-Grilled, Spiced Chicken Breast with Garlic, Manchego & Mixed
  Greens Salad

Pork, Steak & Salmon Satay with Mushrooms, Roasted Bell Peppers, Onions & Mixed Greens Salad

Can't decide what to make to please everyone's palate? Go for this dish, which features pork, steak, and salmon.

Soak the bamboo skewers in water for a minimum of 10 minutes before using to prevent the wood from burning.

---

8 ounces pork loin
8 ounces beef loin
8 ounces salmon filet
¼ cup extra virgin olive oil, divided
2 medium yellow onions, sliced
3 cups sliced mushrooms
8 ounces roasted red bell peppers, seeded and julienned
12 ounces mixed greens
⅓ cup Ó House Dressing (see page 156)
Ó SpanAsian Seasoning Mix (see page 158)

---

1   Heat a grill or grill pan.

2   Cut the pork, beef, and salmon into 4 strips each. Thread the pork, beef, and salmon on separate bamboo skewers. Drizzle about 2 tablespoons oil over the satays.

3   Grill, turning once, until medium-rare, about 2 minutes on each side.

4   Heat the remaining oil in a medium sauté pan over high heat. Add the onions, and sauté for 1 minute. Add the mushrooms and bell peppers, and sauté for 2 additional minutes.

5   Place the greens in a bowl, and drizzle with the dressing. Toss well to coat.

[SERVES 4]

PRESENTATION

Place the vegetables on the serving dishes. Top with 2 satays each. Place a small mound of salad beside the vegetables and satays. Sprinkle the entire plate with the Ó SpanAsian Seasoning Mix, and serve immediately.

BEVERAGE PAIRINGS

Sierra Cantabria
Tinto
Rioja, Spain

Bodegas Bretón Criadores
Loriñón Blanco
Rioja, Spain

Salmon Teriyaki Satay with Garlic-Fried Rice & Mixed Greens Salad

This is a very popular dish that's perfect for a casual summer supper. We make our Garlic-Fried Rice with fragrant jasmine rice, which has a perfumy, nutty aroma and flavor.

Soak the bamboo skewers in water for a minimum of 10 minutes before grilling to prevent the wood from burning.

---

1 pound salmon filet, sliced into 8 pieces
¼ cup extra virgin olive oil
Sea salt
Freshly ground white pepper
8 ounces mixed greens
3 tablespoons Ó House Dressing (see page 156)
1 recipe Garlic-Fried Rice (see page 160)
½ cup teriyaki sauce

1. Heat a grill or grill pan.

2. To make the satays, thread the salmon slices on bamboo skewers. Drizzle with the oil, and season with salt and pepper. Grill, turning over once, until medium-rare, about 1 minute on each side.

3. To make the salad, place the greens in a bowl, and drizzle with the dressing. Gently toss to coat.

[S E R V E S   4]

PRESENTATION

Place the Mixed Greens Salad on each serving dish. Place the Garlic-Fried Rice beside it. Arrange the skewers over the rice and drizzle with the teriyaki sauce. Serve immediately.

BEVERAGE PAIRINGS

Juyondai Sake
Yamagata, Japan

Michizakari Sake
Gifu, Japan

Spice-Grilled Ahi Tuna with Garlic-Fried Rice, Mixed Greens Salad & Orange-Sherry Vinaigrette

One loyal guest at our flagship Ó north of Chicago has ordered this dish every time he's visited us—which has been nearly every week for the past 2 years. It's the favorite of many others, as well, and we're hoping now that they have the recipe, they'll still come to see us!

---

2 tablespoons cumin seeds
2 tablespoons coriander seeds
4 (8-ounce) ahi tuna steaks
3 tablespoons extra virgin olive oil
Sea salt
Freshly ground white pepper
½ cup Cumin Dressing (see page 157)
16 ounces mixed greens
¼ cup Orange-Sherry Vinaigrette (see page 158)
1 recipe Garlic-Fried Rice (see page 160)

1 Heat a grill or grill pan.

2 Toast the cumin and coriander seeds in a small sauté pan over high heat. Place in a coffee grinder and grind until fine.

3 Drizzle the tuna steaks with the oil. Rub with the cumin and coriander, and then season with salt and pepper. Grill until medium-rare, about 3 minutes on each side.

4 Warm the Cumin Dressing in a small sauté pan over medium heat.

5 To make the salad, place the greens in a bowl, and drizzle with the Orange-Sherry Vinaigrette. Gently toss to coat.

[SERVES 4]

PRESENTATION

Place the Mixed Greens Salad on each serving dish. Place the Garlic-Fried Rice beside it. Place the tuna atop it, and drizzle with the warm Cumin Dressing.

BEVERAGE PAIRINGS

Garmona Cava
Grand Cuvée
Catalonia, Spain

Alquézar
Moristel
Somantano, Spain

Grilled Andalusian Spice-Rubbed Steak with Sautéed Shrimp & Spanish Potatoes

When looking for an uncomplicated main course that's sure to impress, go for this one. For variation, melt some crumbled Cabrales cheese over the steaks, and then top with the sautéed rock shrimp.

We use hanger steak for this recipe. This often overlooked cut hangs between the rib and loin. Streaked with fat, it's extremely flavorful and juicy when prepared correctly.

6 (8-ounce) hanger steaks
Sea salt
Freshly ground black pepper
2 tablespoons extra virgin olive oil
3 cloves garlic, sliced
12 ounces rock shrimp
1 tablespoon Ó SpanAsian Seasoning Mix (see page 158)
3 tablespoons minced parsley, divided
12 ounces mixed greens
½ cup Ó House Dressing (see page 156)
1 recipe Spanish Potatoes (see page 157)

1   Heat a grill or grill pan.

2   Lightly season the steaks with salt and pepper. Grill the steaks to your desired doneness. Tent loosely with aluminum foil to keep warm.

3   Heat the oil in a small sauté pan over high heat. Add the garlic and shrimp, and sauté until the shrimp are cooked through, about 2 minutes. Season with the Ó SpanAsian Seasoning, and sprinkle with 2 tablespoons parsley.

4   Place the greens in a bowl, and drizzle with the dressing. Gently toss to coat.

[SERVES 6]

PRESENTATION

Place the Mixed Greens Salad on each serving dish. Place the Spanish Potatoes beside it. Place the steak atop the potatoes, and cover with the shrimp. Garnish with the remaining parsley.

BEVERAGE PAIRINGS

Sapporo Reserve Beer
Sapporo, Japan

Denshu Sake
Aomori, Japan

Quick Tip: Working with Hanger Steak

Like other cuts of beef, hanger steak, when prepared incorrectly, can be tough.

The secret to perfectly moist and tender steak of any type (as well as game) is to allow your meat to rest at room temperature for 25 minutes before cooking, and then to allow it to rest for several minutes before cutting it.

When meat is refrigerated, it constricts, and all the blood is preserved in the center. Cooking meat straight from the refrigerator thus results in a tough, dry piece of meat. When meat rests at room temperature prior to the cooking process, the juices distribute evenly throughout the cut, which makes the tissue soft and yields a tender presentation. Juices also collect in the center during the cooking process, and allowing meat to rest after it cooks enables the juices to redistribute.

Asian Salmon Steak with Mushrooms, Mixed Greens Salad & Garlic-Fried Rice

This light and tasty salmon steak is sautéed with garlic, pickled sushi-style vinegar, and sliced button mushrooms, and then deglazed with soy sauce. Served with a simple salad and our Garlic-Fried Rice, it's a beautiful presentation.

4 (8-ounce) salmon steaks
Sea salt
Freshly ground white pepper
¼ cup extra virgin olive oil
4 cloves garlic, sliced
¼ cup sliced pickled sushi-style ginger
8 ounces sliced button mushrooms
1 cup soy sauce
12 ounces mixed greens
½ cup Ó House Dressing (see page 156)
1 recipe Garlic-Fried Rice (see page 160)
Chopped flat-leaf parsley for garnish

1   Pat the salmon dry with paper towels. Season with salt and pepper.

2   Heat the oil in a large sauté pan over high heat. Add the salmon, skin side down, and sauté until medium, about 5 minutes on each side.

3   Add the garlic, ginger, and mushrooms, and sauté until the mushrooms are tender, about 2 minutes. Deglaze the pan by adding the soy sauce and scraping the bits in the bottom of the pan. Remove from heat.

4   Place the greens in a bowl, and drizzle with the dressing. Gently toss to coat.

[SERVES 4]

PRESENTATION

Place the Mixed Greens Salad on each serving dish. Place the Garlic-Fried Rice beside it. Place the salmon steak atop the rice, and drizzle with the drippings from the pan and the soy sauce. Garnish with the parsley.

BEVERAGE PAIRINGS

Bodegas Nekeas
Vega Sindoa Chardonnay
Navarra, Spain

Ginban Sake
Toyama, Japan

Quick Tip: Fish- and Meat-Turning 101

A common mistake new students at Marcel Biró Culinary School make is turning over their meat or fish before it's ready. So how do you know when it's time? The meat or fish will tell you, because in high-quality cookware, it will release itself from the bottom of the pan when it's perfectly golden brown. You should thus never tear the meat from the pan with your tongs, and note that we specify tongs. Jabbing meat or fish with a fork or knife will create a chimney through which all the flavorful juices will escape.

Desserts

Flan

This is the Spanish version of the French crème caramel, a custard that's baked in a caramel-coated mold. We serve this flan at Ó, as well as sangria and coffee-flavored variations (see below). You'll need six 6-ounce ramekins or oven-proof teacups for this recipe.

2 cups whole milk
½ teaspoon pure vanilla extract
Pinch of ground cinnamon
¾ cup plus 1 tablespoon sugar, divided
¼ cup water
4 large eggs
Whipped cream for garnish
Mint leaves for garnish
Fresh berries for garnish

1 Bring the milk, vanilla extract, cinnamon, and 1 tablespoon of the sugar to a boil in a large saucepan over medium-high heat. Cover, and remove from heat. Allow to infuse for 20 minutes.

2 Preheat oven to 350 degrees F.

3 Place the water and remaining sugar in a heavy saucepan. Cover, and bring to a boil over high heat until the sugar dissolves. Remove cover, and reduce heat to medium-high. Continue to boil, but do not stir, until the mixture becomes syrupy and light amber in color, about 10 minutes. Immediately pour the syrup into the ramekins. Tilt the ramekins so that the syrup swirls up onto the sides.

4 Lightly beat the eggs in a large bowl. Slowly beat in about 1 cup of the milk mixture to temper the eggs. Add this mixture to the rest of the milk. Carefully pass through a chinois or fine-mesh sieve into the ramekins.

5 Place a large baking pan with 2-inch sides in the oven. Place the ramekins in the pan, making certain there's room between them. Create a bain-marie by carefully pouring ½ inch of warm water in the pan. Tent with aluminum foil, and bake for 30 to 40 minutes, or until the flans are just set. Being careful to not splash the water into the flans, remove the pan from the oven. Remove the ramekins from the pan, and allow to cool. You may wish to refrigerate the flans for at least 1 hour before serving, which is a good idea if you plan to invert them onto serving dishes.

[MAKES 6 (6-OUNCE) FLANS]

You may serve flan in the ramekins, which look nice placed on plates and garnished with the whipped cream, mint leaves, and berries. You can also invert the flans onto serving plates. To unmold, carefully run a knife around the edges of the ramekins.

BEVERAGE PAIRINGS

Segura Viudas
Aria Brut
Penedés, Spain

Sandeman
Royal Corregidor
Rare Oloroso Sherry
Jerez, Spain

Quick Tip: Coffee Variation

Drizzle ¾ teaspoon coffee liqueur over the flans before serving. For added visual appeal, flambée—or light afire—the liqueur upon serving. When the flame extinguishes itself, the alcohol taste will have burned off, and all you'll be left with is the great coffee flavor.

Quick Tip: Sangria Variation

Drizzle ¾ teaspoon sangria over the flans before serving. For added visual appeal, flambée—or light afire—the liqueur upon serving. When the flame extinguishes itself, the alcohol taste will have burned off, and all you'll be left with is the great fruit flavor.

Dulce de Leche-Chocolate Tarte Flambée

We use dulce de leche in a variety of desserts at Biró and Ó. It's a Spanish sweet cream that is similar to the sweetened condensed milk widely available in the United States. Here we slather it on a Tarte Flambée Crust, top it with high-quality bittersweet chocolate chips, and cover it with a second Tarte Flambée Crust. Guests always save room for this most popular dessert.

2 sheets Tarte Flambée Crust (see page 160)
4 tablespoons Quark Topping (see page 161)
1 tablespoon dulce de leche or sweetened condensed milk
¾ cup bittersweet chocolate chips
3 tablespoons confectioners' sugar, divided

1 Preheat oven to 450 degrees F.

2 Place 1 Tarte Flambée Crust on a sheet pan lined with parchment paper.

3 Using a silicone spatula or large spoon, spread the Quark Topping over the crust. Drizzle evenly with the dulce de leche. Sprinkle with the chocolate chips and 2 tablespoons of the confectioners' sugar.

4 Place the other sheet of Tarte Flambée Crust over the toppings. Bake for 10 minutes, or until the edges are golden brown. Carefully turn over the tarte and bake for 5 additional minutes, or until the bottom becomes golden brown on the edges. Serve immediately.

[MAKES 1 TARTE FLAMBÉE]

PRESENTATION

At Ó, we serve this dish traditionally, which is on a wooden board. You could use a large sushi board or even a cutting board, carefully sliding the tarte from the parchment paper, and then slicing it into pieces. Garnish with a dusting of the remaining confectioners' sugar. This is a rustic dish, so your guests should feel free to eat it with their hands.

BEVERAGE PAIRINGS

Bodegas Gutierrez de la Vega
Casta Diva Cosecha Miel
Alicante, Spain

Castell Blanch
Semi-seco
Penedés, Spain

Fruit Sushi

Here, strawberry, kiwi, pineapple, and mango are rolled in boton rice sweetened with coconut milk and sugar, and then rolled in chocolate shavings. The result is a fun dessert that looks as good as it tastes.

Fruit Sushi is also great served as an hors d'oeuvre. You'll need a bamboo spoon and mat to prepare this recipe.

3 cups boton rice
4 tablespoons sugar
½ teaspoon sea salt
2 cups coconut milk
8 ounces strawberries, julienned
3 kiwis, julienned
1 small golden pineapple, cored and julienned
1 medium mango, julienned
1 cup shaved semisweet chocolate

1   Rinse the rice in cold water until the water drains clear. Place in a rice cooker, and add the sugar, salt, coconut milk, and water to cover. Allow to rest for 1 hour. Cook the rice according to the manufacturer's instructions. If you do not have a rice cooker, place the rice, coconut milk, and water to cover in a pot, and bring to a boil over high heat. Cover, and reduce heat to low. Cook for 20 minutes, or until most of the liquid is absorbed. Uncover, and cook for 15 additional minutes.

2   Spread the hot, cooked rice on a large plate with a bamboo spoon, and allow it to cool enough to handle.

3   Cover your bamboo mat with plastic wrap to prevent the rice from sticking. Dip your hands in hot water to prevent the rice from sticking to them, and spread about 1 cup of rice evenly over the mat, leaving a 1½-inch border on each long side. Place 4 to 5 fruit juliennes down the center of the mat.

4   Lift the closest end of the bamboo mat up and over the fruit. Press the roll firmly inside the bamboo mat and continue rolling. Transfer the roll to a platter, and remove the bamboo mat. Cover with a damp towel. Repeat with the remaining fruits, and refrigerate the rolls for 30 minutes.

5   Remove from the refrigerator, and roll in the chocolate shavings.

6   Using a sharp knife that has been dipped in water, trim the ends, and then cut the rolls into 8 equal pieces.

[SERVES 8]

PRESENTATION

Serve on wooden boards. You may wish to serve Fruit Sushi with the Chocolate Dipping Sauce on page 133, or with our Raspberry Coulis on page 154.

BEVERAGE PAIRINGS

Fillaboa
Albariño
Rias Baixas, Spain

Montsarra
Cava Brut
Catalonia, Spain

Hojiblanca Olive Cake with Olive Oil Ice Cream

Hojiblanca olives have a sweet, fruity flavor but are fibrous and thus usually not served on their own. They make excellent olive oil, which is fantastic in this unforgettable dessert that's perfect for a Spanish-themed gathering.

If Hojiblanca olive oil isn't available, substitute a high-quality Spanish extra virgin olive oil. You'll need an ice cream maker for this recipe.

3 eggs
Pinch of salt
1¼ cups sugar
Zest of 2 washed oranges
½ cup Hojiblanca olive oil
4 ounces plain yogurt
1¼ cups flour plus more for dusting
Unsalted butter for the pan

ICE CREAM

1 cup heavy cream
2½ cups whole milk
9 large egg yolks
¾ cup sugar
½ cup Hojiblanca olive oil

DISH

Raspberry Coulis (see page 154) for garnish
Fresh raspberries for garnish

1 Preheat oven to 350 degrees F.

2 To make the cake, beat together the eggs, salt, sugar, and zest in a stand mixer until the eggs reach the stiff peak stage. Remove the bowl from the stand mixer. Using a silicone spatula, fold in the oil and yogurt by hand. Carefully fold in the flour.

3 Grease a 9-inch cake pan with the unsalted butter, and then dust with flour. Pour in the batter. Bake for 45 minutes, or until a toothpick inserted in the center of the cake comes out clean.

4 To make the ice cream, prepare the inserts of your ice cream machine as per the manufacturer's instructions.

5 Bring the cream and milk to a boil in a small saucepan over high heat.

6 Meanwhile, place the yolks and sugar in a medium bowl and whisk until the mixture is thickened, fluffy, and pale yellow. You should be able to cover your spoon's back with the mixture and form a rose shape if you blow into it. You may also use a stand mixer fitted with a paddle attachment for this step; it takes about 2 minutes on medium speed.

7 Slowly add about ½ cup of the hot cream-milk mixture to the egg-sugar mixture, and whisk to temper the yolks. Whisking constantly, add the egg-sugar mixture to the cream-milk mixture, and whisk until evenly blended.

8 Reduce heat to medium-low. Using a wooden spoon, continually stir the mixture in figure 8 patterns, making certain that you are involving all the mixture on the bottom and in the corners of the pan. Cook until the mixture has thickened to a coating consistency, 8 to 10 minutes.

9 Fill a large bowl halfway with ice water. Place a medium stainless steel bowl in the ice water, and carefully pour the cream into the bowl. Stir occasionally to cool.

10 Pour the cooled cream into the bowls of your ice cream machine, and process according to your machine's specifications, usually 30 to 40 minutes. Halfway through the process, pour in the oil in a slow, steady stream. Serve immediately or freeze until ready to serve, up to 48 hours.

[SERVES 8]

PRESENTATION

Serve cake at room temperature, garnished with the Raspberry Coulis and fresh raspberries. Add a generous scoop of ice cream, and serve immediately.

BEVERAGE PAIRINGS

Mont Marçal Cava Brut Reserva
Penedès, Spain

Bodegas Gutiérrez de la Vega
Casta Diva "Fondillón"
Alicante, Spain

Pineapple-Coconut Arborio Rice Pudding

This decadent dessert has a rich but bright flavor, satiny texture, and tantalizing aroma. We know that after one try, you'll be making it a lot!

This recipe uses Arborio rice, and like in a properly prepared risotto, it will be al dente—softened but with a toothsome bite—in this dish.

Fresh golden pineapple is best for this recipe, but you may also use canned golden pineapple in light syrup. Drain before use.

---

1 cup whole milk
1 (14-ounce) can coconut milk
1 cup Arborio rice
1 teaspoon vanilla extract
1 teaspoon sea salt
½ cup sugar
6 ounces fresh pineapple, cored and diced
½ cup flour
1 to 1½ cups heavy cream
2 egg yolks
Mint leaves for garnish

1 Place the milks, rice, vanilla extract, salt, and sugar in a large saucepan over high heat. Stirring frequently, bring to a boil, and then reduce heat to medium.

2 Stir in the pineapple. Simmer, stirring frequently, for 8 minutes. Stir in the flour, and cook for 5 additional minutes.

3 Stir in the cream and cook, stirring frequently, for 5 minutes. Reduce heat to low, and then stir in the yolks. Cook for 3 additional minutes, adding additional cream as necessary.

[S E R V E S   6   T O   8]

PRESENTATION

Place in serving dishes, and garnish with the mint. Serve immediately.

BEVERAGE PAIRINGS

Huget Cava Grand Reserva Brut
Penedès, Spain

Lustau
Muscat Emilin
Jerez, Spain

Basic Recipes

Bouquet Garni

2 outer leek leaves
6 sprigs parsley
12 black peppercorns
1 Turkish bay leaf

Lay out 1 leek leaf. Place the parsley, thyme, peppercorns, and bay leaf onto the leek, and lay the remaining leek on top of it to form a cigar-shaped bundle. Tie the bouqet securely with kitchen twine.

[MAKES 1 BOUQUET GARNI]

Raspberry Coulis

1 pint raspberries
2 to 3 tablespoons superfine sugar

1   Place the raspberries and 2 tablespoons of the sugar in a food processor or blender, and purée. Add more sugar, if necessary.

2   Pass the puréed berries through a chinois or fine-mesh sieve to remove the seeds. You may need to add a little water to thin the coulis.

3   Place in a fine-nozzled squeeze bottle, and refrigerate for up to 2 days.

[MAKES ABOUT 1/2 CUP]

Ó Yogurt-Dill Vinaigrette

2 cups plain yogurt
2 tablespoons chopped dill
Sea salt
Freshly ground white pepper

Place all ingredients in a bowl, and using a silicone spatula, mix well to combine. Use immediately, or refrigerate for up to 48 hours.

[MAKES 2 CUPS]

Pesto-Marinated Chicken Breast

1 recipe Pesto (see below)
4 boneless, skinless chicken breasts
Sea salt
Freshly ground black pepper

1   Place the Pesto in a large bowl. Add the chicken breasts, and marinate in the refrigerator for at least 2 hours, and preferably overnight.

2   Heat a grill or grill pan.

3   Grill the breasts until cooked through, 3 to 4 minutes each side. Season with salt and pepper.

[MAKES 4 CHICKEN BREASTS]

Velouté

1½ tablespoons unsalted butter
1½ tablespoons flour
1 cup cold Chicken, Fish, or Vegetable Stock (see pages 152 and 153)
Sea salt
Freshly ground white pepper

1   Melt the butter in a small saucepan over medium-low heat. Whisk in the flour and cook until it just begins to color, about 2 minutes.

2   Pour in the cold stock. Whisking constantly, bring to a boil. Season with salt and pepper.

3   Simmer, uncovered, for 10 minutes, being certain to whisk occasionally and to skim off any impurities that may rise to the surface. The sauce is done when the flavor of flour is no longer apparent and it coats the back of a spoon. Serve immediately, or dot with 1 tablespoon butter to prevent a skin from forming. Refrigerate for up to 48 hours.

[MAKES 1 CUP]

Pesto

3 large garlic cloves
½ cup pine nuts
⅔ cup grated Parmesan cheese
1 teaspoon sea salt
½ teaspoon freshly ground black pepper
3 cups loosely packed basil
⅔ cup extra virgin olive oil

1   Place the garlic in a food processor, and finely chop. Stop the motor, and add the nuts, cheese, salt, pepper, and basil; process until finely chopped.

2   With the motor running, add the oil in a slow, steady stream to emulsify. Process until well combined.

[MAKES ABOUT 3/4 CUP]